SAVING THE BUFFALO

SAVING THE BUFFALO

ALBERT MARRIN

SCHOLASTIC NONFICTION
an imprint of
SCHOLASTIC

For the McMahan grandchildren: Ruth, Ashley,
Everett, Alexander, Gia, Joelle, and David

LIBRARY OF CONGRESS CATALOGING-IN-PUBLICATION DATA
Marrin, Albert. • Saving the buffalo / Albert Marrin. • Includes
bibliographical references and index. • ISBN 0-439-71854-6 •
1. American bison—Juvenile literature. • 2. American bison hunting—
History—Juvenile literature. • I. Title. •
QL737.U53M227 2006 • 599.64'3—dc22 • 2005051827

10 9 8 7 6 5 4 3 2 1 06 07 08 09 10

Printed in Singapore 46
First printing, October 2006
Book design by Nancy Sabato

CONTENTS

CHAPTER ONE

LORD OF THE GREAT PLAINS

Few animals invoke the power and drama of the American buffalo, or bison. Over the centuries since the arrival of humans on the continent, the American Indian peoples of the Great Plains took their living and based many of their customs and religious beliefs on this animal. Today, scores of places bear its name. The Buffalo River, for example, flows through western Tennessee. Three states—Nebraska, South Dakota, and Wisconsin—have counties named Buffalo. Buffalo, New York, is among the Empire State's largest cities. Once the buffalo roamed in such immense herds that we can

A herd of buffalo at a Great Plains lake. Since permanent lakes are rare on the Plains, the one shown here was probably formed by spring rains, only to evaporate during the scorching summer months. Dated 1855, this painting is by John Mix Stanley.

This 1889 map illustrates the extermination of the American bison. It is by William T. Hornaday, a pioneer in the movement to preserve America's wildlife heritage.

hardly imagine them today. Truly the "Lord of the Plains," the buffalo had few natural enemies and, until white people came, none that threatened its existence. Yet white hunters nearly wiped out the buffalo within fifteen years, from 1870 to 1885. The story of the buffalo, how it lived, and how American Indians lived with it is part of our national heritage. So is its near-extinction, the ways it was saved, and its future.

The buffalo's homeland is the Great Plains. These vast open spaces perfectly suit an animal that needs thirty pounds of food a day to eat and miles of land to roam. At the heart of North America, the Plains reach southward from Alberta in Canada into northern Mexico. They extend westward from the Mississippi and Missouri rivers to the Front Range, or eastern slopes, of the Rocky Mountains. Today, parts of ten states are on the Plains: Montana, North Dakota, South

Dakota, Wyoming, Nebraska, Colorado, Kansas, New Mexico, Oklahoma, and Texas. Covering an area of 1.25 million square miles, the Plains are larger than the combined territory of Western Europe, with the British Isles added for good measure.

Land of the big sky. The Great Plains are so flat in places that sky and earth seem to meet in a straight line, as they do in this photo of low-hanging storm clouds.

Apart from northern Texas, also called the Texas Panhandle, the Plains are not perfectly flat, as the name suggests. They slope gently downward, rolling wavelike from the Rockies toward the east. Once the bed of a vast inland sea, they owe their slope to the soil and stones washed down from the Rockies by rain and melting snow; about half the original mountain range has already washed away, or eroded. Over millions of years, the force of water rushing downhill dug deep valleys. Rain and wind then cut into the valley walls to form steep-sided cliffs. Trees, mostly cottonwoods, grow along the banks of the Missouri, Yellowstone, Platte, and other Plains rivers. Otherwise, the Plains are treeless. In a few places, high hills rise sharply from the surrounding lands. Millions of years ago, molten rock bubbling up from the earth's core formed the Black Hills of South Dakota and the Crazy Mountains of Montana.

Plains weather ranges from delightful to dreadful, and everything in between. Although mild and dry for much of the year, the wind is always blowing, often as forcefully as at the seashore. In summer,

Run, fly, dig, or die. This rule about living things and fire on the Great Plains is depicted in this exciting 1888 painting by Meyer Straus.

scorching winds whip out of the Sonoran Desert of Mexico. These send temperatures soaring to 130°F (54°C) in the shade, withering plants and drying up streams. Funnels of dust, nicknamed dust devils, swirl hundreds of feet into the air, creating midnight at midday.[1]

From early fall to early spring, Arctic winds called northers can send the temperature diving fifty degrees within minutes. The blizzards they bring, nicknamed the grizzlies of the Plains (for they are as fierce as these bears), can drop a foot of snow an hour and go on for days. Cloudbursts, lightning storms, hailstones, and tornadoes also batter the Plains. Firestorms, ignited by lightning and driven by wind, burn until they run out of fuel or reach a natural barrier, like a river. Plains fires reach speeds of twenty-five miles an hour, forcing every creature in their path to run or fly, dig or die. However, fire serves an essential purpose; to stay healthy, the Plains need to burn from time to time. Fire clears dead vegetation and produces ashes that return minerals to the soil and helps seeds sprout more quickly. Finally, in a region that seldom gets more than twenty inches of rain a year, droughts may last for years.

Rainfall decides the kinds of grasses that grow in any given area. The Plains have short varieties. While tall grasses flourish on the prairies east of the Mississippi because more rain falls there, across the river on the Plains, the grasses are stunted. The Rockies to the west allow only a few rain-bearing clouds to drift inland from the Pacific Ocean. Blue grama and buffalo grass, the most common shortgrasses, thrive despite scarce rainfall and frequent firestorms. Because their roots are concentrated close to the surface of the soil, they absorb water quickly. Although fire destroys their leaves, it does not reach their roots. Once the flames pass, shortgrasses quickly produce a fresh growth.

Grass was life on the Plains. Before the 1840s, when white settlers first crossed the Plains in large numbers, the place teemed with elk, deer, and jackrabbits, animals that rely on speed to escape predators. Yet, for speed, none touched the pronghorn antelope. Herds of pronghorn bounded across the Plains. Weighing less than one hundred pounds, each adult had long, muscular legs, a large heart, and oversize lungs that allowed it to go up to fifty-five miles an hour. Prairie dogs, a type of ground squirrel, lived in underground "towns," some covering hundreds of square miles and containing millions of animals. Flocks of wild turkeys abounded.

Predators seldom went hungry on the Plains. Golden eagles glided overhead, their keen eyes searching for prey; their shadow on the ground was enough to make prairie dogs scurry into their tunnels. Grizzly bears fed on the living and the dead; in 1831, James Ohio

TOP: Adapted by nature to survive on dry, open grasslands, a healthy pronghorn antelope can easily outrun any predator, including a pack of wolves.

BOTTOM: Young black-tailed prairie dogs playing outside their burrow. Numbering in the tens of millions, these tiny rodents once played a vital role in maintaining the ecology of the Great Plains.

Pattie, a fur trapper, counted 220 grizzlies in a single day. Wolves and coyotes were too abundant to count. These ferocious animals ran in packs of as many as seventy members. European travelers said wolf packs, because of their light coats, resembled flocks of sheep.

A basic law of nature is that, in any ecosystem, everything connects to everything else. An ecosystem is a community of living beings, including humans, that depends on one another in various ways and interacts with its environment. Mountains, rivers, lakes, deserts, beaches, swamps, and seas—to name a few—each contain unique ecosystems. In the Great Plains ecosystem before the arrival of white people, the buffalo was not only the largest animal. It was also what scientists call the keystone animal, the one that others depended on most for their survival.

Plains creatures owed much to the buffalo, and it to them. Grazing herds of buffalo stirred up the soil with their hooves. This pushed seeds into the ground, where they could take root and sprout, becoming food for all grazing animals. Prairie dogs could not live in tall grass. However, grazing buffalo kept the grass to the tiny creatures' liking. In digging their vast underground towns, prairie dogs brought fresh, mineral-rich soil to the surface, increasing the land's fertility. In return, buffalo got needed salts by licking up dried urine around prairie dog holes.

Built for self-defense, the horns of a mature male buffalo can easily make short work of any predator, while the mat of thick, curly hair on its head can withstand a collision during mating contests.

The buffalo made circular holes called wallows by rolling around in damp soil to cool off during the summer. Wallows collected rainwater, forming tiny ponds that supported various plants, insects, small animals, and birds. Dark birds, called buffalo birds, perched on the buffalo's back. As the buffalo walked, the birds dove for insects disturbed by the buffalo's movements through the grass. Buffalo dung, or chips, littered the Plains wherever the herds passed. These lumps of digested grass were tiny worlds, homes to beetles, fly grubs, worms, and molds.

Everything the buffalo did influenced life on the Plains. Even its death had importance. Every decaying body fertilized the soil, while buzzards, bugs, coyotes, and molds fed on it. In short, countless animals and plants owed their existence to the buffalo.

Hot and plagued by insects, these buffalo have twisted their bodies to form wallows in damp soil. Notice how the Plains are not perfectly flat, but gently "roll." Artist George Catlin painted this scene from life around 1837.

CHAPTER TWO

BUFFALO BASICS

The Lord of the Plains belongs to the same family as cattle, oxen, goats, and sheep—all of which feed on grass. The American buffalo, also called the bison, is smaller than the African Cape buffalo and the Asian water buffalo. Its closest relative is the European bison, also known as the wisent; a handful of these still exist in Poland. Just how the word "bison" came to mean "buffalo" in North America is a mystery. The early French explorers of Canada called them *les bœufs*, that is, oxen or cattle. Later, it seems, the English pronounced the word *bufflo*, *buffelo*, and, finally, *buffalo*. To avoid confusion, we will use "buffalo" throughout this book.[2]

A bison on the alert. Despite its large eyes, the bison's vision is poor. It relies on its keen sense of smell to find food and alert it to danger.

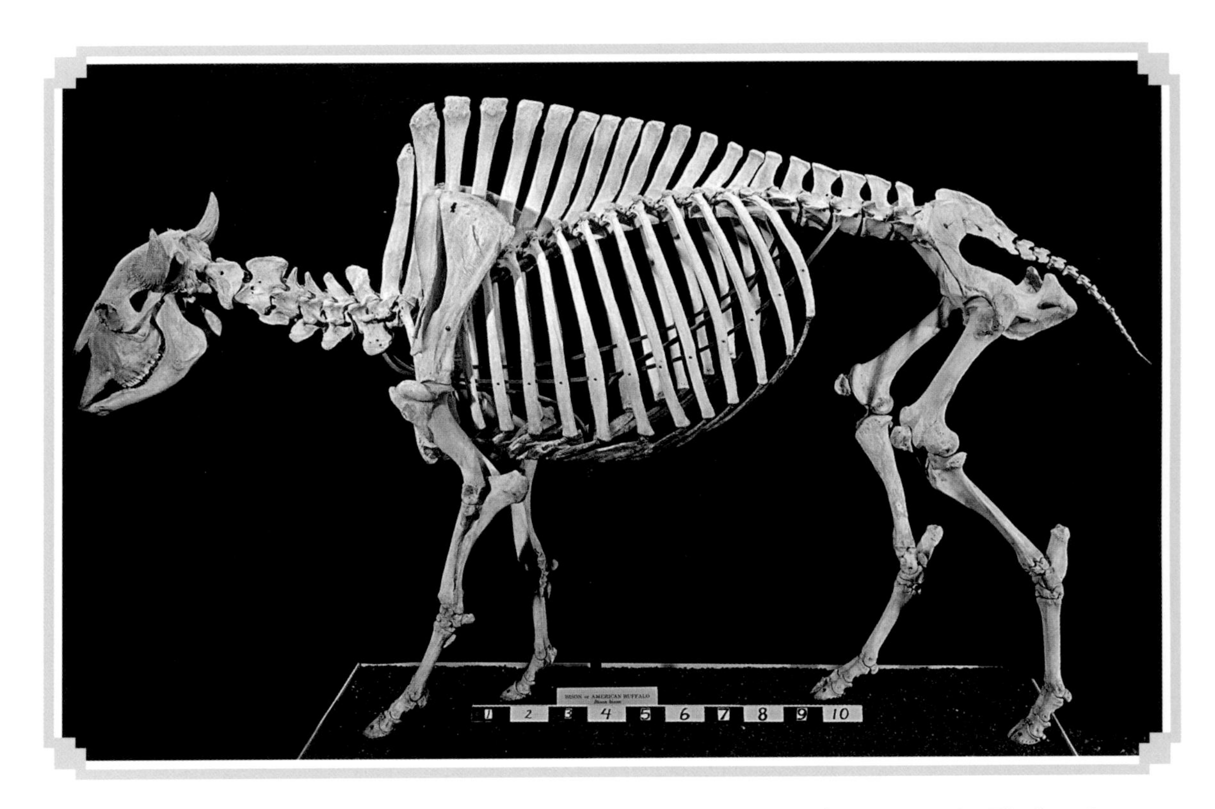

This mounted buffalo skeleton is in the Smithsonian Institution in Washington, D.C. The long bones rising from the front of its spine support its hump. For protection, the bones forming the front of its skull are extra thick—so thick that rifle bullets might bounce off if they struck at an angle.

By whatever name, the buffalo was not the first of its kind in North America. A giant ancestor roamed from the banks of the Mississippi River to the shores of San Francisco Bay on the Pacific Coast. Weighing more than three thousand pounds, it got its Latin name *Bison latifrons,* or "wide forehead," from its wide skull and long horns. A pair of these horns measured up to nine feet in length. Although "wide forehead" died out twenty thousand years ago, its relatives developed into the modern buffalo.

When Europeans first reached North America, the buffalo had an enormous domain. Although centered in the Plains, its territory extended from the eastern base of the Rockies to the Atlantic Coast and from Mexico into Canada.

The largest land animal on the continent, an adult bull stands seven feet at the shoulder, is twelve feet long, and weighs up to two thousand five hundred pounds. In other words, he weighs a half-ton more than any moose or brown bear, the next largest animals. A mature cow is smaller. She stands just five feet at the shoulder, is seven feet long, and can weigh up to one thousand two hundred pounds; her average weight is seven hundred fifty pounds. Although the buffalo has poor eyesight, it can detect sudden movements a mile away. Its hearing is excellent, as is its sense of smell.

When not sleeping, the buffalo spends most of its time eating. Like its relatives, it is a ruminant, that is, an animal with a stomach divided into four compartments. To digest tough plant fiber, ruminants chew it, swallow it, pass it to the next compartment, bring it up, and repeat the process. Always on the move, the buffalo roams its range, going at most several hundred miles in any direction. While doing so, it seemingly follows no pattern, or has any regard for the season. In the wild, it lives from twelve to fifteen years, though some may live to twenty.

Before white hunters, seasonal changes were the buffalo's worst

This adult bison bull is much larger than the adult cow.

enemy. The coldest winter did not faze it. Well-fed animals had layers of fat and thick coats of hair to insulate them against the worst northers. When the wind blew hardest, they turned toward it, standing still or walking into it. Thus, the storm passed quicker for them than if they had traveled ahead of it. In deep snow, they pressed their noses downward until they sniffed grass, then swung their heads back and forth to clear the snow away. However, after a blizzard, bright sunlight

Although snow might cover a buffalo from head to tail, thick layers of fat prevent it from losing body heat during the coldest winters.

might turn the top of the snow into slush. When the temperature dropped at night, the slush froze, forming a crust of ice. If the crust remained hard, the buffalo could not feed.

Ice was the true killer of buffalo in the winter. Should they wander onto smooth lake or river ice, they might fall and slide around, breaking legs or hips. In early spring, as the ice thinned, they might break through and drown. Melting ice and snow filled rivers, turning them into raging torrents. Caught in the current as they tried to swim across, buffalo drowned by the thousands.

Quicksand along the riverbanks claimed thousands more. A fur trapper once counted 7,360 drowned buffalo in the quicksand beside a Canadian river. "In one or two places," he wrote, "I went on shore and walked from one carcass to the other, where they lay from three to five files deep." In the distance, other travelers saw a herd standing perfectly still. Moving closer, they found that the animals had gotten stuck in mud. While the buffalo struggled to get out, the mud must have hardened around their legs, holding them fast. The buffalo starved to death; then the wind and sun mummified their bodies, preserving them as lifelike as the day they died.[3]

In summer and autumn, lightning struck individual buffalo, burning off every bit of hair. Tornadoes lifted dozens of others high into the air, then slammed them into the ground, breaking all their bones. Once, after a tornado, travelers found hundreds of twisted bodies stacked in heaps four and five deep.

Fires took a heavy toll, too. In 1804, Alexander Henry, a fur trapper, described the effects of a fire in his diary: "Plains burned in every direction and blind buffalo seen every moment wandering about. The poor beasts have all the hair singed off, even the skin in many places is shriveled up and terribly burned, and their eyes are swollen and closed fast. It was really pitiful to see them staggering about, sometimes running afoul of a large stone, and other times tumbling down hill and falling into creeks, not yet dead. In one spot we found a whole herd lying dead." Blind buffalo, however, were not necessarily helpless. Blindness often sharpened its sense of hearing and smell, making it super-alert to danger. To eat, it merely had to follow the scent and sound of its herd, grazing as it went.[4]

In comparison to seasonal dangers, predators did little harm. Now and then a grizzly bear killed an aged buffalo. Pound for pound, however, a grizzly was no match for a healthy buffalo. Wolves were far more aggressive. We might think that buffalo would run away if a wolf pack came close, but they did not. Normally, they paid little attention to wolves, even letting them pass among them. This was probably because, over thousands of years, they had gotten to know wolf habits pretty well. Wolves were not always hunting, so were not always a

Although their eyesight is poor, when they smell danger, like this pack of wolves, buffalo bulls form a protective circle around the herd's young. In this drawing, from Harper's Weekly, *August 5, 1871, the wolves cannot get past the slashing horns.*

threat. Besides, buffalo seemed to know that wolves seldom attacked an individual standing close to a herd. However, if attacked, a buffalo close to its herd could depend on the others for help. Young bulls surrounded calves, their heads lowered, their horns pointed outward. These horns could make short work of any wolf. Thus, wolves attacked only those they caught alone—usually the young, the old, and the sick.[5]

A buffalo can run when it wants to. The muscles attached to its hump allow it to lengthen the stride of its front legs, increasing its speed. An adult can run thirty-five miles an hour, and keep running for five miles; a racehorse can run forty miles an hour, but tires after just a mile. Almost anything can set off a stampede—a dry leaf blowing along the ground, a distant flash of lightning, or a coyote's howl. The instinct to stampede is a means of self-defense. It allows a herd to leave an area quickly. Also, with so many animals running in the same direction, a predator cannot easily focus on a single animal. The rumbling sound of a stampede carries for miles, and the ground shakes. Any living thing in its path aboveground faces certain death. In their wild rush, buffalo in the rear might overtake and trample those ahead of them. Spanish explorers once saw a stampede in Texas. "They trampled one another until they came to a ravine," a Spaniard wrote. "So many of the animals fell into this that they filled it all up, and the rest went across on top of them."[6]

A high-strung creature, the buffalo's first reaction to anything unusual is to break into a run, as in this stampede. The herd will keep running until exhausted or halted by a stream or other natural barrier. Some white observers said a stampeding herd would suddenly stop, because the buffalo forgot why they were running.

For most of the year, cows and bulls lived in separate groups of between twenty and fifty. Cow groups had adult cows, calves, and young bulls; bull groups had mature bulls. In summer, when the new grass was most nutritious, the groups joined for the rut, or mating season. As temperatures soared, the animals shed their heavy winter coats. Hair came out in bunches, exposing bare skin to hot sun and biting flies. Until their summer coats grew in, the buffalo

Buffalo calves grazing with their mothers. Should they get separated in the herd, each calf has its own call and smell, enabling its mother to tell it apart from countless look-alikes.

wallowed in cool, wet holes for relief. They made holes by rolling their bodies around on patches of damp ground. When they stood up, the clinging mud dried into a sunburn- and insect-proof shell. When the shell wore away after a few days, they made more wallows.

Both genders have horns, but a bull's horns are thicker than a cow's and curve upward. Horns begin as buttons on a calf; on a bull a pair of horns can reach a total of thirty-five inches in length. Bulls use their horns for grooming, defense, and fighting for the privilege of mating. During the rut, they test their strength by charging, slamming their heads together, and pushing against one another. The momentum built up by two thousand pounds of buffalo moving at thirty-five miles an hour was terrific. "The muscles on thighs and hips rose like huge welts," an English traveler wrote. "We could see the roll of their blood-red fiery eyes. . . . The froth began to drip in long strings from their mouths.

Bison love dust as well as mud. The dust clouds they kick up protect them from biting insects—at least for a short time.

They were both panting, their tongues lolling out."[7] Yet bulls seldom drew blood, much less died in these battles. Their thick skulls easily absorbed the shock. Finally, the weaker bull, sensing defeat, ran away.

After mating, the herds again broke into small groups and lived apart for the fall, winter, and early spring. Calves were born in the spring. And then it was summer—time for the next rut.

When the groups combined in late spring and summer, buffalo moved in immense herds. European travelers who later saw the herds could hardly believe their eyes. Even today, their written accounts astonish us. For example, in the 1830s, a Christian missionary declared the buffalo were "in number—numberless." Twenty years later, a hunter following the Platte Valley in Nebraska wrote:

Picture in your mind a grassy valley a mile wide and straight for many miles, level as a floor, bare

As is typical of buffalo, this herd in South Dakota sticks close together when it moves.

The first white people to picture the bison never saw it in real life. Living in Europe, they based their pictures on the accounts of the early Spanish travelers across the Plains. This one, dating from the 1550s, is from the General History of the Indies *by the Spaniard Francisco Lopez de Gomara, who was given his information from Cortés and other explorers of the New World.*

of any trees and brush. . . . . Early one morning in 1851, I stood on an eminence [hill] overlooking this valley. . . . [It] was literally blackened with a compact mass of buffalo. . . . And not only this—the massive bluffs on both sides were covered by thousands and thousands that were still pouring down into the already crowded valley, and as far as the eye could see, the living dark masses covered the ground as completely as a carpet covers the floor. It looked as if not another buffalo could have found room to squeeze in, and a man might have walked across the valley on their huddled backs as on a floor. This herd was on the move and was many hours in passing.

Elsewhere, a writer swore he saw a herd covering 1,350 square miles, an area larger than the state of Rhode Island![8]

How many buffalo were roaming the Plains really? We cannot be sure. The best scientific guess—and it is just a guess—is that between 30 million and 65 million buffalo lived when Christopher Columbus reached the Americas in 1492. By then, hunting the buffalo had become vital to the lives of certain American Indian peoples.

A front view of a stampeding buffalo herd.

CHAPTER THREE

HUNTING ON FOOT

American Indians had hunted buffalo for more than ten thousand years before Europeans set foot in North America. The earliest Plains dwellers were nomads, wanderers living among the buffalo herds as best they could. Their legends tell of the Plains as a land of mystery and beauty, of dread and hardship. They say that enormous mythical birds, called Thunderbirds, lived in the spaces between the stars. Masters of storms, these birds had flashing eyes that sent lightning zigzagging earthward, turning dry grass into an inferno. The beating of their wings brought blasts of wind and cloudbursts; the hatching of their eggs made thunder. There was also the Giant of the North, bringer of

Like the Shoshone pictured here, Plains Indians lived in tents made of tanned buffalo hide. The woman at right is pegging a fresh buffalo hide on the ground to dry. Cooking pots hang over fires made of chips, lumps of dried buffalo dung.

winter. His very breath froze the earth hard as rock and sent blizzards.[9]

Besides hunting the buffalo, the early Plains dwellers ate any other meat that came their way, including beaver tails, birds' eggs, and grasshoppers. Whenever possible, they gathered edible roots, prairie turnips, wild plums, wild onions, and many other types of plants. Over the centuries, through trial and error, they learned to use various plants to treat wounds and illnesses.

Since nomads had no permanent homes, they could not have many possessions—and nothing heavy. It was hard to follow the buffalo closely, as the herds constantly moved to new grazing grounds. Sometimes an Indian band camped near a herd, only to wake up the next morning and find that it had drifted away during the night. Scouts might then have to search for days until they found it or another herd. Thus, nomads always lived between extremes, between prosperity and starvation. After a good kill, they gorged, filling their bellies until they bulged. Then they went hungry until the next kill, which might be days or weeks away.

Without any sort of wheeled vehicles, nomads traveled on foot, covering perhaps six miles a day. Armed men walked ahead, to lead the way and protect their families. Each woman might carry a baby or a bundle on her back, holding a toddler by the hand. The rest of the family's possessions rode on a travois, or "dog-drag," a wooden frame slung between two long poles, the ends tied to the shoulders of a dog. Descended from wolves captured as puppies, these half-wild creatures constantly fought among themselves and snapped at people. At most, each dog could pull a travois with a thirty-pound load.

Plains nomads lived in buffalo-skin tents for most of the year, but in winter they sheltered in river valleys. Although they were protected from northers, with a good water supply nearby, hunger still pinched their bellies. Food saved from the warmer months seldom lasted the winter. Thus, they called winter "the time when our babies cry for food." If they were lucky, they killed buffalo disabled on slippery ice or trapped in snowdrifts. To get around in snow, hunters wore snowshoes

Blackfoot hunters on snowshoes pursuing buffalo. While the big animal's legs sank into deep snow, making escape difficult, snowshoes had a larger surface area, allowing the hunter to walk atop the snowdrifts.

made of thin wooden frames with plant-fiber webbing. As February turned into March, though, people weakened by hunger began to die. Scientists have found evidence that entire bands starved to death during the severest winters.

About a thousand years ago, some Plains nomads learned about agriculture, although how is a mystery. We do know that Pueblo peoples to the southwest—Hopi, Zuñi, and Taos—lived in stone "apartment" houses built into cliff walls overlooking rivers. Able

A Hopi pueblo, or village, built into the side of or atop a steep cliff. Expert farmers, the Hopi and other Pueblo peoples traded their produce with hunters for buffalo meat. Before the coming of the European settlers, American Indian trade routes extended all the way from the Mississippi River to the Pacific Ocean.

farmers, the Pueblos dug irrigation canals to bring water to their fields of maize, beans, squash, and sunflowers. We also know that Plains nomads traded buffalo meat to the Pueblos for farm products. Perhaps they learned agriculture from them. However it happened, nomadic peoples like the Apache and Navajo settled down on the western fringes of the Plains from Texas to the Rockies. Combining gardening and gathering, they became part-time buffalo hunters. Meanwhile, the Three Tribes—Hidasta, Mandan, and Arikara—settled along the upper reaches of the Missouri River in what is now North Dakota. Living in solidly built homes of sun-dried clay and thatch, they planted large fields of vegetables. Yet they still loved buffalo meat.

Come spring, as the ice on the Missouri River cracked, villagers gathered along the banks to recover buffalo that had fallen through and drowned. After days in the water, the carcasses had begun to decay. No matter. Charles McKenzie, a trader visiting the Mandans, reported: "When the skin is raised [removed], you will see the flesh of a greenish hue, and ready to become alive [with insects] at the least exposure to the sun; and is so ripe, so tender, that very little boiling is required." It made a "delicious" green soup.[10]

Meanwhile, men and women prepared their fields. Working together, they cleared away last year's stalks, pulled weeds, and planted seeds. To prepare for the buffalo hunt, they set fire to the Plains nearby.

This may seem reckless, given the severity of firestorms, but was usually safe. With the ground damp from spring rains, there was little chance of a runaway fire. Nature, too, had taught them a valuable lesson about fire. They noticed that land blackened by fire behaved differently from unburned land. It felt warmer to the touch, because black absorbs sunlight readily. Somehow, this made the new grass come up two to three weeks earlier than on unburned land. The savory new growth attracted buffalo, making it easier to get meat earlier.

At the start of summer, as the crops ripened and the herds massed for the rut, villagers made medicine. For American Indian peoples, medicine had two meanings. It meant healing the sick. Yet, above all, it was a way of talking to the spirits. Indians believe that everything has a spirit. Living beings have spirits, as do the things of the earth and the forces of nature such as wind, fire, and earthquakes.

Making medicine involved sacred ceremonies. Such ceremonies acted out whatever people wished to happen later. Before a hunt, farmer-hunters performed the buffalo dance to attract their prey and persuade its spirit to surrender its body to them. Since the spirit never dies, they thought, it would return in the form of another buffalo, a guarantee that the herds would never diminish.

In the 1840s, artist George Catlin saw a buffalo dance in a Mandan village. He wrote:

Karl Bodmer painted Bison-Dance of the Mandan Indians *in 1840. The Mandan were farmers who lived in permanent villages and hunted only part-time. Like most American Indian peoples, they believed that acting out a hunt might later make the real hunt a success. Here we see "buffalo," men wearing buffalo heads, resisting "hunters" armed with spears and rifles.*

About ten or fifteen Mandans at a time join in the dance, each one with the skin of the buffalo's head (or mask) with the horns on, placed over his head, and in his hand his favorite bow or lance, with which he is used to slay the buffalo. . . . Drums are beating and rattles are shaken, and songs and yells incessantly are shouted. . . . When one becomes fatigued . . . he signifies it by bending quite forward, and sinking his body towards the ground; when another draws a bow upon him and hits him with a blunt arrow, and he falls like a buffalo—is seized by the bye-standers, who drag him out of the ring by the heels. . . . Having gone through the motions of skinning and cutting him up, they let him off and his place is at once supplied by another, who dances in the ring with his mask on; and by this taking of places, the scene is easily kept up night and day, until the desired effect has been produced, that of "making buffalo come."[11]

Before a hunt, excitement gripped a village as older children caught the family's dogs. Mothers packed the travois and fathers checked their weapons. The very young and the very old stayed behind with a few strong women to look after them and the crops. The hunting grounds were not very far, perhaps a hundred miles at most.

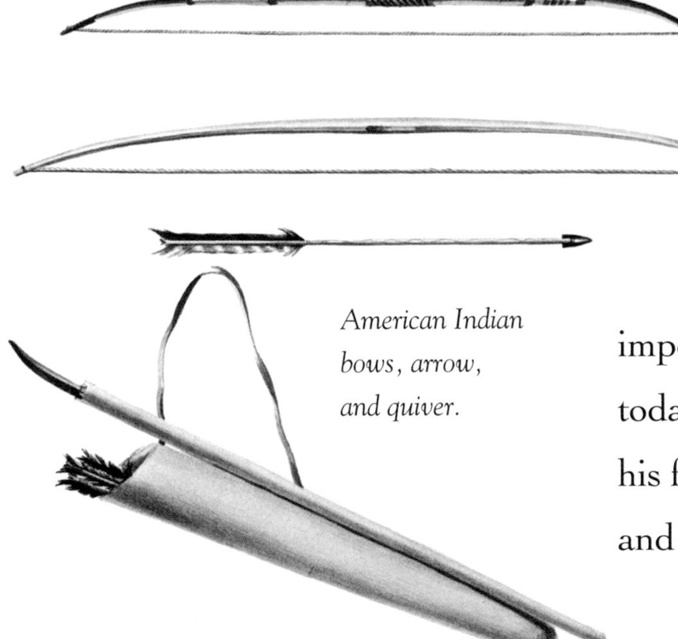

American Indian bows, arrow, and quiver.

Hunting was a vital skill, as important as reading and writing are today. A boy began learning to hunt when his father gave him a small set of bow and arrows, and taught him to use them.

As he grew, becoming more expert with practice, his lessons included tracking game. To locate a moving buffalo herd, for example, he must put his ear to the ground to feel the vibrations of distant hooves. By examining dung, he could tell from its shape, contents, and warmth what animal left it, what it had eaten, and if it was nearby. Most of all, he studied animals' habits and figured out how to get close enough to kill them.

Hunters used the buffalo's own instincts and habits against it. Since a herd allowed wolves to come close, a hunter covered by a wolf skin, crawling on all fours, could shoot an arrow from just a

A Blackfoot warrior's headdress of buffalo hair and eagle feathers. Only an accomplished warrior had the right to wear such a splendid headdress. He could shoot more arrows faster, farther, and more accurately than any white man could shoot bullets with a gun in the 1840s.

few yards away. This was fine, but produced only a few buffalo kills at a time. The object of a village hunt, however, was to kill the most within the shortest time. To do this, everyone had to act as part of a team.

Teamwork took various forms. If the wind was right and the danger of a firestorm slight, hunters made a fire surround. Moving cautiously, without showing themselves, they surrounded a herd and ignited the grass. However, they left a few unburned exits, where hunters waited to ambush the panicked beasts. If the wind shifted and the fire spread, hunters joined the buffalo in a mad dash to escape. The problem was that the hunters could not go very fast, or very far, on two legs. Now and then, an out-of-control fire reached a camp, trapping scores of men, women, and children.

Impounding was safer than the fire surround. Each family wedged its travois upright in the ground in two lines that branched out in a long V shape. The top of the V was about a mile wide. The point of the V opened onto a place with a five-foot drop, a kind of corral enclosed by rocks or tree trunks. If there was no natural drop, the men dug a steep-sided pit.

Everybody crouched behind the travois-screens. Occasionally, excited children raised their heads to see what was going on, only to be yanked back by their mothers. What they saw might have seemed funny, had it not been so important.

George Catlin's Buffalo Hunt under the Wolf-skin Mask. *In this 1832 painting, the famous artist shows a method of buffalo hunting that dates back to the time before Plains Indians rode horses. Even after they became riders, hunters might don wolf skins and act like wolves to surprise a grazing herd.*

Buffalo grazed in the distance, beyond the spreading arms of the V. Nearby, an experienced hunter, called the buffalo-caller, or chaser, or He-Who-Brings-Them-In, crouched on his hands and knees. A buffalo skin covered his body; he wore a hollowed-out buffalo head, horns and all, on his own head. The man's every motion and sound, the result of countless hours of practice, exactly mimicked a buffalo's. He snorted. He pawed the ground. He rolled in the dust. He bleated like a calf

In this 1823 engraving, George Back pictures hunters impounding buffalo. His work combines fact and fiction. While hunters did hide until the animals came close enough to strike, they would not build a "pound" so close to their village. With their keen sense of smell, the buffalo would have easily detected the village and run away.

"being devoured by a wolf and crying for help." A European traveler wrote after seeing a hunt, "[his gestures] so closely resembled those of the animals, that had I not been in on the secret, I should have been as much deceived as the buffalo."[12]

Buffalo are inquisitive creatures. The doings of that "buffalo" just ahead soon caught their attention. A cow moved toward it for a better look. Others followed. As they did, the fake buffalo moved farther into the V. He was "bringing them in." Gradually, the entire herd drifted in the same direction, into that funnel of death.

Suddenly, the hidden people rose, shouting and banging weapons together. As expected, the buffalo stampeded. For them, running with the herd had always meant safety. Not now! Within seconds, the caller jumped behind a rock; there was no time to lose. As he did, the first victims had already entered the corral. Trapped, they lunged against the sides, without effect. Some tribes called the corral a *pis'kun*, or "deep blood kettle." It deserved the name. As the people lunged with flint-tipped spears, struck with stone-headed clubs, and shot arrows, the place became awash in buffalo blood.

The most dramatic type of hunt produced the most kills. Known as the buffalo jump, it was like impounding, except that the point of the V opened not to a corral but to the edge of a cliff. With the animals in the rear pushing the others ahead of them, those in front had built up too much momentum to turn or stop. Over they went, tumbling and kicking, bouncing and crashing, against the cliffside. The dead and dying piled up, sometimes ten deep, at the foot of the cliff. Waiting hunters finished off the injured with their weapons.

Scientists have identified more than one hundred buffalo jumps.

Among the largest are Cabin Creek on the Yellowstone River and a cliff overlooking the Chugwater River, both in Wyoming. At Sun River Valley west of Great Falls, Montana, buffalo bones weighing some fifty million pounds cover an area of five acres; in some places, they

are seven feet deep. These could not have accumulated in a few hunting seasons. Indians used these favored spots for countless generations. One buffalo jump has become famous. In 1981, the United Nations declared Head-Smashed-In a World Heritage Site. Lying just south of Calgary, Canada, it holds a protected place in world culture equal to that of the pyramids in Egypt and the Great Wall of China.

ABOVE: *Head-Smashed-In Buffalo Jump. Fort Macleod, Alberta, Canada. Apparently, bison were not the only animals Indian hunters drove off cliffs. In some sites, deer bones have been found along with those of the buffalo.*

LEFT: *Although hundreds of animals might die within minutes at a buffalo jump, a herd's normal birthrate easily made up for the loss. Alfred Jacob Miller painted this scene around 1858.*

No matter how many buffalo they trapped, the hunters made every effort to kill them all, letting none escape. Some writers later faulted them for "recklessness" and "wanton wastefulness," deliberately killing more than they could use. This is totally opposite from the truth. Plains peoples taught, each tribe in its own way, not to waste any part of an animal they killed. "Don't kill more meat than you think you can . . . pack home. That way it won't be wasted and lie around rotting," men cautioned one another. Be "careful to gnaw the bones of the animals so that no meat whatever is left on them." Yet they still left buffalo meat to rot and killed any survivors they could find. Why?[13]

We get a hint in the report of a Canadian fur trader. "When hunting," he wrote, "they take but the fattest . . . part of an animal and [leave] the remainder." Taking only the fattest part made sense and, to Indians, was not wasteful. Over the centuries, they learned from experience that, while they could live on a diet chiefly of meat, they had to eat a certain amount of fat for energy. Of course, they could only learn if an animal was fat enough after killing it. Still, even a lean animal might have some fat in its tongue and hump, which explains why hunters might take only these parts. Hunters also tried to kill every buffalo because they believed those that escaped would warn others to avoid the trap.[14]

As the killing ended, the rest of the camp arrived for the butchering.

A large bull yielded up to nine hundred pounds of meat, plus its hide; a large cow yielded about five hundred pounds of meat. Butchering was hard work, so everyone who could lent a hand.

Families rolled buffalo humps, steaks, and anything else they could use in the skin and hauled it to camp on their backs and travois. That night, there were favorite dishes like blood soup, that is, blood poured into boiling water and thickened with brains. Hooves and tails became soup, too. The buffalo even furnished the pot. Its paunch, the lining of the first of its four stomach compartments, was tough and leathery. Women stretched the paunch over four forked sticks, placed meat, water, and anything else they wished inside, then added heated stones to bring it to a boil. Ten fist-size stones usually did the job. When the paunch-pot became soggy after several uses, they ate it, too.

The Osage people of Oklahoma made this drum of buffalo hide stretched over a wooden frame. Drums like this, decorated with sacred symbols, were used in ceremonies before setting out on a buffalo hunt.

Strips of buffalo meat hang from a wooden rack. When the meat is dry, women will pound them with stone hammers and mix them with dried fruits to make pemmican. The woman shown here wears cloth clothing, a sure sign that her people traded with whites.

Whatever was not eaten was prepared for the winter. Plains Indians had little salt and no spices to preserve meat. That did not matter, for there was plenty of sun and wind on the Plains. Meat was preserved as either jerky or pemmican. Women "jerked" buffalo steaks by cutting them into long strips about a quarter of an inch thick, then hanging these over wooden racks to dry. Jerky was as tough as shoe leather and as tasty, but could last about two years. You ate it as is, chewing mightily, or softened it in a paunch-pot. No matter how it was prepared, Plains Indians had jerky for breakfast, lunch, dinner, and snacks.

Pemmican was ideal for people on the move. Women made pemmican by pounding jerky with stone hammers, then mixing crushed nuts, berries, and wild cherries into the flaky mass, pits and all. After pouring melted fat over the mixture to form an airtight cake, they pressed it into buffalo-skin bags about the size of pillowcases. Pemmican could last thirty years without losing its nutritional value. Removed from its bag, it was tastiest when sliced and dipped in wild honey. White travelers adopted this "Indian bread." Arctic explorers relied on beef pemmican as a lightweight, quick-energy food. Admiral Robert E. Peary, the first person to reach the North Pole, said his men ate it cold—a half-pound twice a day—and enjoyed every bite. During World War II, U.S. Navy lifeboats had pemmican in their survival kits, and German sailors stocked their version of it in their submarines to save space in the cramped vessels.

Plains hunters did not grow cotton and did not raise sheep, so they didn't have raw material for cloth. Instead, they used tanned buffalo skin for everything from moccasins and shirts to blankets and tipi covers. Tanning required strength, skill, and patience. Working together, female relatives and friends stretched a hide on the ground

A Lakota woman uses a bone scraper to clean a buffalo skin stretched on a wooden frame. Later, other women, family members, relatives, and friends will help her tan and soften the skin so she can make it into clothing.

with the flesh-side up, and kept it from curling by securing it with wooden pegs. Using a stone or bone scraper, they removed the fat and muscle, making the skin even. To tan it, they smeared on a paste of boiled buffalo brains and water. For ten days they kept the skin moist with this paste. After that, they rubbed

Tanned and rubbed soft, this buffalo robe was probably made from the hide of a calf and decorated with paintings of horses. The mounted figure in the center seems to be aiming a rifle at a person standing on the ground.

and pulled it back and forth over the edge of a board. Although women made tanned buffalo hides into all types of clothing, they took special pride in their buffalo robes. Worn with the fur on the outside, robes made ideal winter garments.

Indians had nearly a hundred uses for the buffalo besides food and clothing. The rough side of its tongue made an excellent hairbrush. Horns became cups, spoons, and ladles. Since Indians had no matches, they carried smoldering embers long distances protected inside buffalo horns. Strands of buffalo beard decorated clothing and weapons. Hair became paintbrushes, rope, and stuffing for gloves; women wore buffalo-hair bracelets and earrings, too. When twisted, sinew, the long tendons lying along either side of the backbone, provided sewing thread and bowstrings. Bones easily became needles, awls, flesh scrapers, knife blades, and ornaments.

Dating from around 1840, this pipe bag is made of buffalo hide and glass beads. The beads could have come only from white traders, who came to the Plains seeking buffalo robes for sale in the eastern states.

Made of buffalo hide, this Hopi mask represents the sun. Since the Hopi were farmers, the sun was especially sacred to them. The Hopi often traded with Plains hunters, giving corn and squash in return for buffalo meat and hides.

Ribs served as skids for sleds. Boiled hooves produced glue for attaching feathers to arrows. The tail became a whip or a fly whisk. Tied to a circular wooden frame, an entire hide became a bull boat, a watertight craft for rowing two or three people across a river.

Indian women prized buffalo fat as an ingredient in cosmetics. Mixed with yellow bile or powdered clays of various colors, it served as makeup and sunburn cream. Buffalo-Bird-Woman, of the Cree people, told a visitor: "I painted every morning because the wind and air made our faces dark, tanned them as you say, so we painted that our complexions would not darken. . . . To paint my face I rubbed grease made from buffalo back fat into my palms and then rubbed my palms over my face. Then I opened the mouth of the paint bag and with the flat of my three fingers I touched the paint. . . . Of course a little of the paint clung to my fingers which were oily from the buffalo fat. I now touched my fingers, first to one cheek and then to the other, and finally I rubbed the paint evenly on my face."[15]

This portrait of a Blackfoot woman, Crystal Stone, wife of Chief Buffalo Back Fat, was painted by George Catlin in 1832. The red makeup on her face, made of plant dyes mixed with buffalo grease, was worn as a cosmetic and as protection against sunburn.

The buffalo's dung was put to good use, too. Lacking wood on the Plains, Indians used chips for fuel. In rainy weather, the chips kept dry on the inside. When burned, they produced a hot, nearly smokeless fire to warm a tipi or cook a meal. Mothers pounded old chips into diaper powder for their babies. To amuse themselves, youngsters threw buffalo chips at one another.

For century after century, Indians followed the familiar routines of planting, harvesting, and buffalo hunting. Then life changed dramatically. The horse came to the Plains.

CHAPTER FOUR

HUNTING ON HORSEBACK

Horses once lived in North America, but vanished some twelve thousand years ago for reasons that still puzzle scientists. However, beginning with Columbus's voyages, the Spanish not only introduced crops like wheat and barley, and animals like cattle and sheep, to the Americas. Most important, they brought back the horse.

Seventy years after conquering Mexico, in the 1590s the Spanish pushed northward into Pueblo country, into what is today the state of New Mexico. There, settlers set up farms and ranches, forcing local Indians to work for them. In order

Seth Eastman painted The Buffalo Hunter *around 1858. To shoot his arrow, the hunter must use both hands, letting go of the horse's reins. The horse has been trained to respond to the pressure of the rider's knees against its sides.*

Nicknamed the Cowboy Artist, Charles M. Russell was a Texas cowboy who painted scores of pictures depicting aspects of life in the old West. In The Buffalo Hunt, *he shows how close mounted riders must get to buffalo in order to be most effective with a lance or bow and arrow.*

to manage their cattle herds, the Spaniards trained Indian men as cowboys, or *vaqueros*.

Overworked and mistreated by the ranchers, scores of Pueblo cowboys fled each year. To avoid capture, they went to live with the Apache, farmers and buffalo hunters but also daring warriors. In return for protection, the fugitives brought gifts of stolen horses and taught the

Apache to ride. Soon the Apache were breeding horses on their own. As their horse herds grew, they traded spare mounts to neighboring Indian peoples, sharing their horse knowledge as the *vaqueros* had done with them.

With each passing year, horses spread across the Plains, as one group after another learned to ride. By 1776, as the American Revolution raged in the thirteen colonies, nearly forty peoples had given up farming to become horse Indians. Some of these were new to the Plains, coming from as far away as the Front Range—the mountains closest to the Plains—of the Rockies and the forests bordering the Great Lakes. Among them were the Cheyenne, Comanche, Lakota (Sioux), Crow, Gros Ventre, Plains Cree, Blackfoot, Arapaho, Kiowa, Pawnee, Shoshone, and Assiniboin.

These horse Indians shaped their societies around hunting the buffalo. "The buffalo was part of us," said a Lakota wise man named Lame Deer. "It was hard to say where the animal ended and the man began."[16]

Lame Deer was right. Plains peoples, particularly the Lakota, saw the buffalo as a teacher and benefactor. Lakota legend says that during their wanderings, the people were hungry, for the buffalo had not yet appeared on earth. Then one day, they met a beautiful woman who changed into a white buffalo, then back into a woman. White Buffalo Woman, as they called her, taught Lakota women all they needed to

Medicine Buffalo of the Sioux, *by George Catlin. Like all Plains Indian hunters, the Sioux, or Lakota, believed that the buffalo was "medicine"—that it had supernatural powers. Appealing to its spirit, they believed, might encourage the herds to offer them their bodies for food, clothing, and shelter.*

sustain the family. She taught boys and men about honesty, generosity, and courage. The day after she left, buffalo herds appeared, covering the Plains as far as the eye could see.

Plains peoples believed buffalo and humans could talk to one another, even turn into one another. People took buffalo names, such as Big-Female-Buffalo, Suckling-Buffalo-Calf, and Two-Buffalo-Heads. The most famous Indian with a buffalo name was Sitting Bull, the Lakota spiritual leader and warrior who fought the U.S. Army in the 1870s. Men painted buffalo heads on their faces; boys had the backs of their heads shaved, leaving only a buffalo "tail" dangling. People might even fall in love with buffalo, as in the Lakota tale of "The Man Who Married a Buffalo." When people died, they went to a spirit land filled with buffalo to hunt.

Every Plains Indian buffalo hunt followed a set pattern. It began with a religious ceremony, for hunting was not just a matter of killing for a meal. The night before the hunt, each hunter prayed to the buffalo's spirit, asking it to surrender its body

Sitting Bull, the famous Lakota holy man and warrior, holds a pipe with a stone bowl. Known as catlinite, the stone is reddish brown, believed to represent the blood of all American Indians. Certain pipes were considered sacred and used in religious ceremonies.

A buffalo surround on horseback. As George Catlin shows in this painting, a surround was fast-paced and dangerous. A hunter in the middle has been thrown from his horse and is trying to escape by running over the backs of the tightly packed herd. The hunter in the foreground has also been thrown and is trying to catch his white horse.

to them willingly. "Grandfather, my children are hungry. So I must kill you," he would say. And if he did kill, he apologized to the animal's spirit, honoring it with prayers for the "buffalo nation."

Next morning, at daybreak, the hunters checked their weapons and painted their horses, as they painted their own bodies, with magical symbols to bring luck and avoid harm. Then, riding five abreast, they left camp in a solemn procession. As they did, they sang a sacred song:

I go to kill the buffalo.
The Great Spirit sent the buffalo.
So give me my bow; give me my bow;
I go to kill the buffalo.[17]

Hunting was a community effort, in which each member acted for the common good. The basic rule was "Do nothing to scare away the buffalo." No one could ride out ahead of the group, since that might alert the herd, spoiling everyone's chances. Special officers, called dog soldiers, enforced the rule. These men had absolute power, and used it without hesitation. If anyone dashed ahead, dog soldiers knocked him off his horse, whipped him with a buffalo-tail whip, broke his weapons, and even killed his horse. If he still resisted, they might kill him, too.

What Plains Indians called buffalo-running was unlike older methods of hunting, such as luring the animals into traps or driving them over cliffs. Mounted hunters simply overpowered their prey in a short, fierce charge.

Cautiously, the hunters gathered along one side of the buffalo herd, making sure to stay downwind so it would not get their scent until the last moment. Everyone, men and horses, was restless. While waiting for the chief's signal to charge, the hunters leaned over to whisper in their horses' ears. "Do not fear the mighty buffalo, my friend." "Steady. Be brave." "Run fast." Specially trained for hunting, these horses needed no encouragement. They knew what was about to happen and were eager to get going.

When everyone was in position, a holy man puffed on a sacred pipe. Slowly, solemnly, he blew red willow-bark smoke toward the sky, toward the four directions, toward the earth, and toward the buffalo. "*Hoka hey!*" the Lakota chief shouted. "Charge!"

The horses sprang forward. They ran, an old-time hunter recalled, "as if their hearts were glad."[18]

"*Hopo!*" hunters cried at the top of their voices. "Let's go!"

Sensing danger approaching, the buffalo stampeded. By then, it was too late. The hunters rode into the midst of the herd, shooting arrows and thrusting with their fourteen-foot lances.

Buffalo-running was dangerous, high-speed work. A galloping

A buffalo bull butts a horse, knocking its rider to the ground while the rider's companion moves in for the kill with a lance. From a painting by George Catlin.

George Catlin's Buffalo Bull: A Grand Pawnee Warrior, *1832. Buffalo Bull wore his personal symbol—the head of a buffalo bull—painted on his face and chest. He also wore a large medal, most likely a gift from the U.S. government as a sign of his authority among the Pawnee.*

horse might step into a hole, breaking a leg and throwing its rider, who might break his neck. An enraged buffalo might lift its attackers off the ground on its horns, tossing hunter and horse over its back. Or it might suddenly turn its head, slicing open a horse's belly with its horns, sending guts gushing out.

Artist George Catlin witnessed a buffalo-running. It left him thrilled, stunned, and shaken.

[The buffalo], becoming infuriated with the deadly wounds in their sides, erected their shaggy manes over their blood-shot eyes and furiously plunged forward at the sides of their assailants' horses, sometimes goring them to death at a lunge, and putting their dismounted riders to flight for their lives. . . .

Some who were closely pursued by the bulls wheeled suddenly around and, snatching the part of a buffalo robe from their waists, threw it over the horns and eyes of the infuriated beast and, darting by its side, drove the arrow or the lance into its heart. . . . I sat in trembling silence upon my horse, and witnessed this extraordinary scene, which allowed not one of these animals to escape out of my sight.[19]

Despite the risks, on a good day a band of hunters could easily kill three hundred buffalo in a running that lasted ten minutes. A running would not last much longer than that, because Indian horses lacked the stamina to go more than a mile or two at top speed. After butchering the buffalo, Indians always made sure to leave a bit of flesh as an offering to their Great Spirit.

Scientists believe that horse Indians killed no more than 450,000 buffalo in any given year, a number easily replaced by the calves born each spring. This is a key fact. For it means that North American Indians in no way threatened the buffalo's existence. Then came the strangers from where the sun rose, from the east. These invaders of the Great Plains—white settlers, soldiers, railroaders, hide hunters—would change everything. Not only would they bring the buffalo to the brink of extinction, they would threaten the Indians' entire way of life.

OFFICE
RAILWAY COMPANY
OFFICES.
C.W. HAWKINS,
TAXIDERMIST
K.P.R.W.
KANSAS PACIFIC
DENVER

CHAPTER FIVE

THE WAR ON THE BUFFALO

America's first white settlers had little interest in the buffalo. Buffalo were not profitable like cattle, whose meat Europeans had always enjoyed. The English colonists thought buffalo a nuisance. These lumbering beasts got in the way, trampling crops and competing with their farm animals for grazing. So, whenever buffalo were found, they were shot. After the American Revolution, as land became more costly in the eastern states, more pioneers moved westward. Life was hard for them, and food scarce until they could clear the ground of trees and plant a crop. To tide them

Some "sportsmen" preferred to buy rather than kill their trophies. Displayed in a town along the Kansas Pacific Railroad, mounted buffalo heads like these sold for about one hundred dollars each. In the 1870s, fashionable people hung animal heads as decorations in their homes.

At first, white settlers thought buffalo chips disgusting. However, they soon learned to prize them as fuel on the treeless Plains. This Kansas woman has gathered chips in a wheelbarrow, probably enough for a day's cooking.

over until the harvest, they lived on buffalo meat. Thus, by 1832, the buffalo had vanished everywhere east of the Mississippi River, but still roamed the Plains in the millions.

In the 1830s, hats made of beaver skin became fashionable in America and Europe. White trappers began working Plains rivers and streams on the eastern slopes of the Rockies, where the animals built their dams, or nests. These mountain men often lived with Indian bands, marrying Indian women. When it came to the buffalo, the Indian was their teacher. They learned to make bull boats to cross streams. To get drinking water, if necessary, they would slit open a buffalo's belly and drink the liquid that gushed from its paunch. Trappers also drank melted fat by the quart; unlike cattle fat, buffalo fat did not upset the stomach—or so they said. Like Indians, they savored buffalo intestines, particularly the mush of partially digested grass they contained.

By the 1840s, heavy trapping nearly wiped out the beaver in the West. Meanwhile, fashion changed, as makers of men's hats began substituting sealskin for beaver. Now fighting for their economic lives, trappers had to change with the times. Some left the West, finding different work as best they could. Others turned to the buffalo for their living.

Back east, where most whites lived, the 1840s saw a rising demand for buffalo tongues and robes. Restaurants served buffalo tongues as delicacies. Easterners used robes as blankets in wagons, buggies, and sleds. Plains peoples produced about one hundred thousand robes a

A buffalo hide yard, Dodge City, Kansas, 1878. About forty thousand hides are piled in a long mound taller than a man. Workers in the background at the left use a special device to compress hides into bundles for easy transportation by railroad.

year, which was just about all their women could make to sell and still meet their families' needs.

In exchange for these products, whites traded guns, ammunition, iron knives and arrowheads, sugar, coffee, mirrors, glass beads, woolen blankets, tobacco, and colorful cotton cloth. So-called "Indian whiskey," however, was the most profitable item of all. A pint, which cost a penny to make, could buy a beautiful buffalo robe that sold for twenty dollars in New York City. Some Indians became addicted to this drink—an addiction thought to be as strong as one to heroin and cocaine.

Plains Indians, who dealt only with white traders, had no idea how many whites there really were. All they knew was that the strangers came from far away, from where the sun rose each morning. But in 1843, the first wagon trains left Independence, Missouri, on the Oregon Trail. Instantly, the Plains peoples and the buffalo became part of the larger story of American history.

Free farmland in the Oregon Territory drew white settlers westward. Fewer than a thousand used the trail in its first year. Each family in a wagon train had its own prairie schooner, a large wagon covered with canvas, glistening white as a ship's sails. Although they seemed too few for the Indians to worry about that first year, things quickly changed. Each following year brought a tidal wave of humanity. In 1849 alone, more than forty thousand people, fifty thousand cattle and oxen, and twelve thousand wagons came along the trail. Indians could hardly believe their eyes. A Lakota chief watched, amazed, as wagon trains rolled past his camp for a solid week. Finally, he pointed eastward and asked a settler: "Are there still any whites remaining there?"[20]

As their wagon trains crossed the Plains, white settlers left behind garbage, discarded furniture, and cattle carcasses. The constant rumbling of wagon wheels and the gunfire of eager whites scared the buffalo herds away from the main trails. This, in turn, forced American Indian hunters to travel farther for game.

Although the wagon trains were still crossing the Plains only on the way to somewhere else, the travelers changed the face of the land. In the river valleys, they cut all the trees for firewood. Their prairie schooners' iron-rimmed wheels bit deeply into the land, leaving ruts visible even today. Settlers left campsites with heaps of trash and fouled water holes. For mile after mile, broken-down wagons and discarded furniture lined the trail.

Yet, in the early years of the westward movement, settlers found stretches of the trail "literally covered with buffalo," so that "tens of thousands were to be seen at one view." With the trail blocked, wagon trains stayed put until the buffalo passed, which might take days. That soon changed.[21]

The buffalo began to suffer. Settlers' horses, cattle, and oxen ate the grass for miles on either side of the trail—grass the buffalo needed for grazing. As Indians had known for centuries, buffalo learned from experience. Before long, their grazing patterns changed. Herds began to avoid the Oregon Trail, grazing far to the north and south of it. That, in turn, was bad news for the Plains peoples. Scouts would ride hundreds of miles from camp, only to return without sighting their prey. Prayers and dances failed to bring the herds back to their old ranges. To get food, hunters had to ride farther and search harder than ever before. In doing so, they met other peoples doing the same, triggering wars over hunting grounds.

While traveling across the Nebraska plains, settlers like these would have discarded extra furniture and left heaps of garbage beside the trail.

In the 1850s, a new type of hunter discovered the Plains. Describing themselves as gentlemen hunters, these wealthy Europeans took advantage of the rapid travel offered by steamship, to visit once-remote places. Hungry for adventure, they shot lions and elephants in Africa, tigers in Asia, and polar bears in northern Canada. Upon returning home, they boasted of their exploits, proudly displaying the heads of their prey on their living room walls.

Dr. William T. Hornaday, a naturalist who would later help save the buffalo from extinction, had no use for gentlemen hunters. "Give him a gun," Hornaday wrote, "and something which he may kill without getting himself in trouble, and, presto! he is instantly a savage . . . finding exquisite delight in bloodshed, slaughter, and death, if not for gain, then solely for the joy and happiness of it."[22]

This description fit Sir George Gore perfectly. An Irish nobleman, Gore owned thousands of acres of prime farmland, which brought him a huge income from rents paid by his tenants. Growing tired of following the hounds—following his pack of dogs on horseback until they caught

Whites hunting buffalo for sport. The man on the left uses a rifle, while his companion blazes away with a pistol. The idea was to kill as many buffalo as possible within the shortest time.

a fox and tore it to shreds—he decided to go after buffalo. Money was no object. Gore spent a half-million dollars on a single expedition, an amount equal to nearly eleven million dollars in today's money.

In the spring of 1854, Gore left St. Louis, Missouri, on the first leg of a three-year hunt. He traveled in style, with 40 servants, 112 thoroughbred horses, 50 hunting dogs, and 24 oxen to pull his 6 wagons. Three cows gave him fresh milk. Gore slept in a large linen tent with green and white stripes. The tent covered a brass bedstead and Oriental rugs. By the time Gore finished, he had shot 2,500 buffalo, 1,600 elk, deer, and antelope, 105 grizzly bears, and countless smaller animals.[23]

Gore was not the only hunter, but he was one of the flashiest of the gentlemen hunters. Yet even they did not threaten the buffalo's survival. The real slaughter was to come. Its cause would be a combination of greed and technology.

When the American Civil War ended in 1865, the nation began to build transcontinental railroads. Gone were the days of the Oregon Trail and those like it farther south, such as the Santa Fe Trail. The "Iron Horse" took their place. Within a decade, lines of gleaming steel track stretched across the continent, linking the Atlantic with the Pacific Coast three thousand miles away. Railroads opened the heartland of the continent to settlement. Towns grew up beside the tracks to service the trains and the settlers who began to farm cheap, often free, government lands. Before the railroads, white Americans could not settle on the Plains, because they had no way to get their crops to distant markets. Now they could.

Like the wagon trains before them, the railroads met the buffalo. The "shaggies" and "stinkers," as construction workers called them, were a nuisance. When, for example, the Atchison, Topeka, and Santa Fe line was being built across central Kansas, buffalo herds covered the Plains. Buffalo raced trains, sometimes running so close that passengers could reach out and touch them. Suddenly, animals on one side of the track would try to cross to the other, ahead of the speeding train. "Each individual buffalo went at it with the desperation of despair," said a newspaper report, "plunging against or between locomotive and cars, just as the blind madness chanced to take them." Herds derailed trains. In trying to scramble over

Railroads offered special low-cost tours to encourage "sportsmen" to hunt buffalo on the Kansas plains. Although a few choice cuts of meat might be taken from the carcasses, most dead buffalo were left to rot where they fell. Frank Leslie's Illustrated Newspaper, *June 3, 1871.*

cars, some animals caught their legs in broken windows. Engineers gave up first. They began to bring their trains to a screeching halt when a herd seemed intent on crossing the track. Although the herd took its own sweet time, even a day or two, it was better to wait than to have to set overturned cars back on the track. The buffalo could so damage a railroad car that it had to be abandoned.[24]

Still, railroads could not do without the buffalo. Laying track was hard physical labor, and workers built up mighty appetites. The companies hired professional hunters to shoot buffalo to feed the work crews.

The champion hunter was an unemployed Civil War veteran named William F. Cody. In 1867, the Kansas Pacific Railroad (later renamed the Union Pacific) hired Cody, at a salary of five hundred dollars a month, to provide buffalo meat. He was twenty-one years old. With his trusty rifle, which he named Lucretia Borgia, Cody would shoot buffalo from horseback. One day, while chasing a wounded bull, his horse, Brigham, stumbled, sending him flying. Legend has it that some soldiers nearby laughed, teasing him with a jingle:

Buffalo Bill, Buffalo Bill,
Never missed, and never will;
Always aims and shoots to kill
And the company pays his buffalo bill.[25]

The name stuck, but he had the last laugh. In eighteen months, Buffalo Bill shot 4,280 buffalo. His exploits made him a celebrity with newspaper readers in places like New York and Boston. He started a circus, Buffalo Bill's Wild West, to dramatize life on the frontier. It made him rich.

Portrait of Buffalo Bill Cody as a dapper showman. He leans on Lucretia Borgia, his favorite rifle during his days as a hunter for the Kansas Pacific Railroad.

Railroads popularized the buffalo, too, putting it into the sights of anyone who could afford a rifle and a train ticket. For ten dollars, the cost of a round-trip ticket, companies offered the thrill of the kill, but in complete safety and comfort. Twice a week, trains left St. Louis, Chicago, and other cities, bound for "buffalo land." Some trains carried as many as three hundred passengers, including women. Their only purpose was to shoot buffalo, or to watch others do it.

Awful as this was, the railroads exposed the buffalo to a still greater peril. They provided a cheap way to ship buffalo hides east for tanning.

Advertisement for W. E. Webb's book, Buffalo Land. *Books like this were sponsored by railroads. By promoting easy, cheap transportation, they encouraged whites to come west to hunt buffalo, go into ranching, and build new cities.*

In 1871, a Pennsylvania tannery, followed by tanneries in Germany and England, discovered how to turn buffalo hide into high-quality leather. Overnight, once worthless flint, or raw buffalo hide, sold for $3.50 each. This was big money, compared with the dollar a day, or less, a factory worker earned at this time. Thus, technology triggered the greatest slaughter of big land animals in recorded history.

It began in Kansas. With its railroad depot and warehouses, one town, Dodge City, was the perfect jumping-off point for buffalo country. Hunters could buy supplies in Dodge, then set out to make their fortunes. Hidemen, as they called themselves, were mostly young, between the ages of seventeen and thirty. Although they came from different backgrounds, they had one thing in common: All hoped to get rich quickly. Some were misfits, unable to find a place in the workaday

Street scene in 1878, during the early days of Dodge City, Kansas. Called the "wickedest town in the West," Dodge City hosted buffalo hunters, cowboys, saloon keepers, gamblers, and shootists, gunmen who lived by breaking the law or by enforcing it. Bat Masterson, the famous gunman and lawman, began his career as a buffalo hunter.

world. Others were fleeing unhappy marriages, city slums, and the law. Many had "forgotten" their true names. Instead, they went by nicknames: Shoot-'em-up Mike, Light-fingered Jack, Shotgun Collins, Prairie Dog Dave, Dirty-face Jones. A scruffy, smelly lot, they might go months without a bath. In describing a typical hideman, a Texas lawman wrote: "He had long hair and was the dirtiest, greasiest, and smokiest mortal I had ever seen."[26]

For hidemen, buffalo hunting was as much a team effort as it was for Plains Indians. A hunting team included a shooter, five or six skinners, and a cook who served as a jack-of-all-trades. Their gear was basic: a wagon, whiskey, flour, canned beans, rifles, bullets, grindstones, and a supply of wicked-looking butcher knives. The buffalo they killed provided more meat than any team could eat in a year.

The team's boss was the shooter. Each morning, he left camp alone. His weapon made it unnecessary to get very close to his prey. The Sharps buffalo gun, manufactured by the Sharps Rifle Company of Hartford, Connecticut, was specially designed for shooters. It cost one hundred fifty dollars, had a telescopic sight, weighed sixteen pounds, and fired a cartridge a half-inch in diameter, the same size later used in antiaircraft machine guns. It was able to down a buffalo at three quarters of a mile. Astonished Indians said the Sharps "shoots today and kills tomorrow."

Unlike the Plains Indians and Buffalo Bill, the shooter did not chase buffalo on horseback. Although exciting, this method was impractical, because it scattered bodies over a large area. The shooter wanted them concentrated, making it easier for the skinners to do their work. After all, time was money on the buffalo range.

The shooter took cover behind rocks or clumps of grass. His object was to make a stand, that is, to keep the buffalo from fleeing, while

In George Catlin's Bison Hunt, *three whites hiding in a gully prepare to shoot at a grazing herd. It is probably the rutting season, since the two pairs of males are butting heads.*

shot them one by one. Patiently, he studied the herd, searching for the leader, usually an old cow. Then, placing his rifle in a rest made of a forked stick, he took aim and squeezed the trigger. *BANG!* A sharp noise echoed across the Plains, followed by a puff of smoke. A buffalo fell. The others came up, sniffed the body, but stayed where they were.

Why didn't they stampede? We can't be sure. But some scientists think the answer may lie with the buffalo's familiarity with its environment. Herds were used to loud bangs and puffs of smoke on the

Plains. The shot from a Sharps rifle sounded like distant thunder, which signaled rain. Rifle smoke resembled dust devils, clouds of windblown dust. Since neither signaled death to the buffalo, it had no reason to flee. Similarly, death was no stranger to the herds, due to age, sickness, and wolves. Whatever it was that made the buffalo stay, a shooter might kill as many as two hundred fifty in a single stand.

When the shooter finished, the skinners got busy. Working in pairs, they loosened the hide from the underlying flesh and tied a corner to a horse. A crack of a whip made the horse jerk backward, tearing off

Buffalo skinners at work. Covered with blood and unable to bathe unless camped near a river, these men smelled so bad that they constantly attracted insects and itched so much that they rubbed themselves raw. Townspeople called them stinkers, after the popular nickname for the buffalo.

In 1874, George Robertson photographed this hunting camp in the Texas Panhandle. The hunters have stretched their "green," or new, hides out to dry on the ground. Buffalo tongues, a delicacy in eastern restaurants, hang on the rack to the right.

the hide, leaving the carcass. Back in camp, they pegged the hide to the ground, Indian-style, to dry.

Returning to Dodge City at the end of the hunting season, each team dumped its hides in great mounds, often taller than any man, beside the railroad tracks. Buyers from tanneries went from mound to mound, examining the goods and paying cash on the spot. Workmen then loaded the hides onto eastward-bound trains. Between 1872 and 1873, some 3.2 million hides were shipped out of Kansas. Yet this figure is nowhere near the actual number of buffalo killed. Historians believe that only one in four hides ever reached market. Careless handling, decay, and insects ruined the rest. Thus, hidemen probably killed 12.8 million buffalo within a year. New births could never make up for such a gigantic loss.[27]

Plains peoples might have called Kansas a gigantic *pis'kun,* a kettle of blood, stretching from horizon to horizon. Within two years, the herds vanished from the state. In the spring of 1874, the hunting teams moved south, into Texas.

Indians quickly realized what this meant for them. Although they lacked the word "keystone," they understood that many other creatures, themselves included, depended on the buffalo. If it was destroyed, they and their entire way of life would perish. Thus, to survive, they believed they must fight.

War parties struck the railroads. They ambushed tracklayers and burned isolated stations. In some areas, trains no longer moved at night, for fear of being derailed by iron bars placed across the tracks. Raiding parties attacked farmers' and traders' wagons. Hidemen got no mercy. Yet, no matter how many died, hunting paid so well that others always took their place.

The U.S. Army got the job of keeping order in the entire Plains area. It had its hands full. In the early 1870s, the Indians seemed to have all the advantages. Trained as hunters and warriors, they fought

An artist's dramatic version of a scene that never happened. Masses of Indians never attacked wagon trains, let alone army wagons, as indicated by the "U.S." stenciled on the one in the foreground. Settlers crossed the Plains armed to the teeth; soldiers also took light cannons along. Attacking wagon trains would have cost too many warriors' lives, thus reducing the number of hunters who provided food.

on their home ground. Marvelous riders, they traveled far, struck fast, and escaped before the enemy caught his breath. Army leaders soon realized that they could never win this kind of war. The usual methods of artillery bombardments followed by mass charges simply did not work on the grasslands.

William Tecumseh Sherman, the army's commanding general, and Philip Sheridan, his deputy, decided to change tactics. Both men had learned their trade in the Civil War. That struggle taught them about total war, that anything that sustains the enemy's ability to fight is fair game. Not only must they defeat enemy soldiers, they must also make enemy civilians suffer as much as possible. The idea was to make innocents so miserable that they would make the fighters give up. Thus, in the American Civil War, Sherman burned Atlanta, Georgia, and Sheridan burned Virginia farms to keep food from the Confederate armies. Now, the Plains Indians would taste the bitterness of total war. In Sherman's chilling phrase, it would "bring the Indian problem to a final solution."[28]

Instead of chasing after Indian raiding parties, army scouts located their villages. Cavalry units then burned the tipis, destroyed pemmican stored for the winter, and turned the people out onto the Plains. As an added blow, they shot all the Indian horses they could find. Yet worse followed. Realizing that the peoples depended so totally on the buffalo, the army waged war on the herds. Soldiers opened fire with cannons when buffalo passed forts; they also stampeded herds over cliffs.

Most important, the army and the hide hunters became allies. Not that the alliance took the form of a signed-and-sealed treaty. The agreement was unofficial. Nonetheless, hidemen knew they could count on the army for whatever they needed, and get it free of charge: supplies, ammunition, even military escorts. With brutal frankness, a fort commander told hideman Frank H. Mayer that killing buffalo was safer than killing Indians, who fought back. "Only when the Indian becomes absolutely dependent on us for his every need," the officer said, "will we be able to handle him. He's too independent with the buffalo. But if we kill the buffalo, we conquer the Indian."[29]

White settlers could make extra money by collecting buffalo skulls and bones. These were shipped to factories and ground into fertilizer.

So the war on the buffalo continued. By 1878, the Texas herds, largest of all, were gone. Meanwhile, the Northern Pacific Railroad had laid its tracks across the Montana plains. Now more than five thousand shooters and skinners moved north. By setting grass fires, they trapped the herds in a triangle of land bounded by the Missouri, Yellowstone, and Musselshell rivers. With buffalo blocked from water and grazing running low, it became almost too easy to kill them. "There was no sport about it, simply shooting down the famine-tamed animals as cattle might be shot down in a barn-yard," a newspaper reported.[30]

Between 1879 and 1883, the Northern Pacific Railroad carried some three hundred thousand hides eastward. Yet we must remember that, for each hide shipped, at least three more buffalo died, making a grand total of 1.2 million. No hides went east after 1885. A similar slaughter had taken place in Canada. Apart from a few survivors here and there, the buffalo had vanished from the Plains. All that remained were decaying carcasses and piles of bones.[31]

Mixed with those bones, some said, were the bones of American Indians. Gone was their main support, and with it the freedom the horse and the buffalo had given them. Forced onto reservations, they lived on government handouts and small-scale farming. Although large, reservation lands were usually so poor that settlers did not want them.

The Indians' pain was more than belly deep. Losing the buffalo left them heartbroken, stunned, and confused. Years later, the Crow chief Plenty Coups would recall that "when the buffalo went away the hearts of my people fell to the ground." Sitting Bull, the Lakota leader, agreed: "A cold wind blew across the prairie when the last buffalo fell—a death wind for my people." But why? Why would any person do such a terrible thing to the buffalo? Black Elk, a Lakota holy man, could only think of one reason—money, or gold. Whites, he declared, "killed them for the metal that makes them crazy. . . . You see that the men who did this were crazy."[32]

Yet not all white people were crazy. For as the end of the buffalo drew near, other whites resolved to save them.

A bison effigy. Carvings like this were used in ceremonies to encourage the buffalo to offer their bodies so the hunters might feed their families.

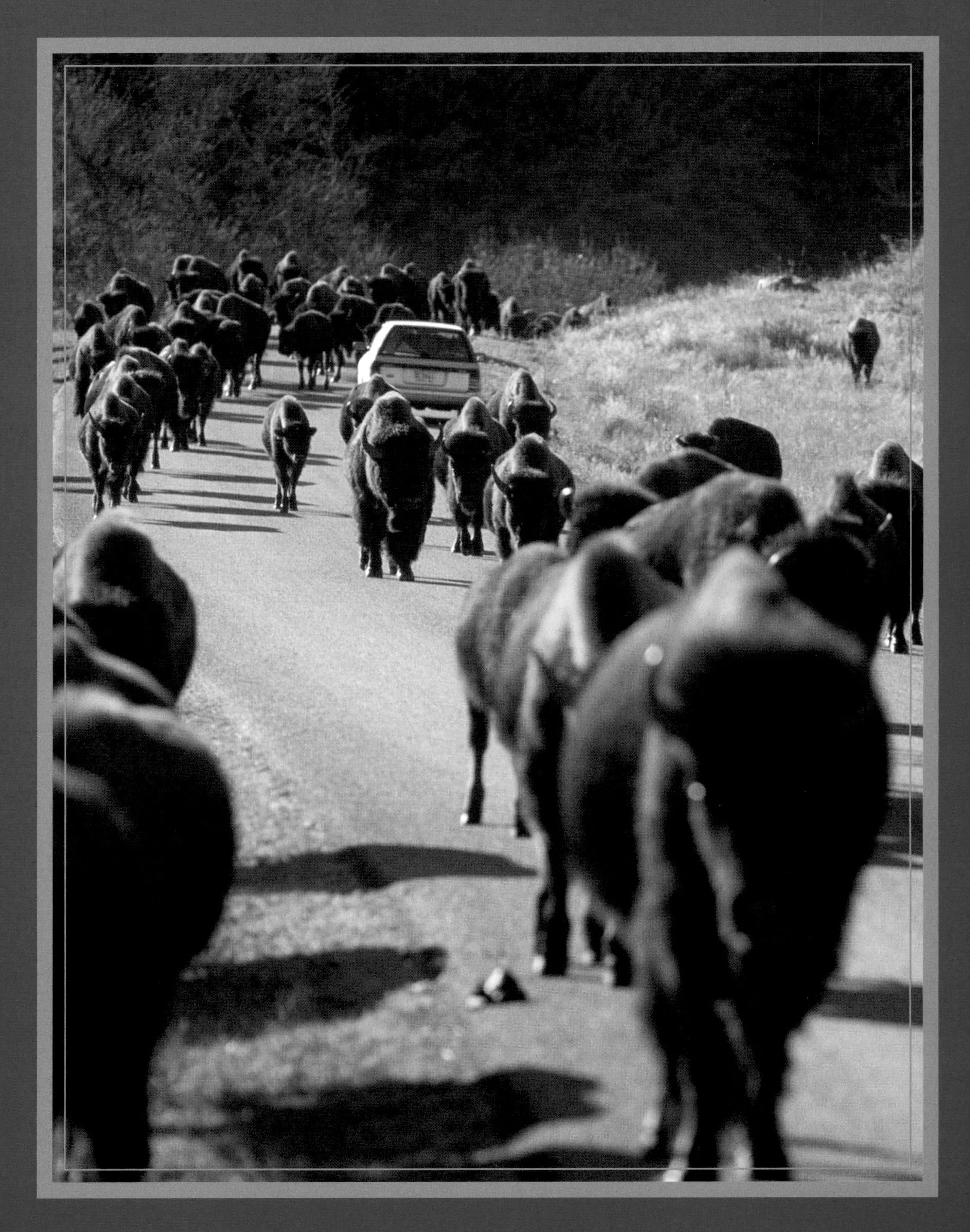

CHAPTER SIX

SAVING THE BUFFALO

Henry Bergh was a tall, skinny string bean of a man. The son of a wealthy shipbuilder, he cringed at the thought of harming any creature. There was plenty to make him cringe. Cruelty to animals was common in Europe and America. Before electrical and gasoline power, horses, mules, and oxen drew all land vehicles except railroad trains. People saw these animals as tools. And, like

LEFT: A buffalo herd shares a road with a car in Custer State Park, South Dakota. People have been gored, even killed, when leaving their cars to snap close-up photographs.

RIGHT: Henry Bergh, founder of the American Society for the Prevention of Cruelty to Animals (ASPCA).

tools, owners used them as much as they could, then threw them away when they " broke." That meant beating work animals to get the most out of them. When they could no longer work, they were left to die in city streets or sold for fertilizer and glue. Owners forced other animals, particularly dogs or roosters, to fight until one died, while onlookers bet on the outcome for entertainment's sake.

Bergh believed that such cruelty brought out the worst in people. Cruelty bred cruelty, so that a person who harmed animals might just as easily harm another person. Kindness toward animals, however, would have the opposite effect. It would make people kinder and more respectful toward one another, he said. So, in 1866, Bergh founded the American Society for the Prevention of Cruelty to Animals. Based in New York City, the ASPCA got laws protecting working animals and pets passed nationwide.

As president of the ASPCA, Bergh also launched a publicity campaign to educate the public about the slaughter of the buffalo. The cruelty of the hidemen, and the waste of meat that could have fed jobless factory workers, outraged Easterners. Bergh also won the support of several army officers stationed on the Plains. Most outspoken was Colonel William B. Hazen, a Civil War hero and commander of Fort Hays, Kansas. Hazen condemned the slaughter as a "wicked and wanton waste, both in the lives of God's creatures and of the valuable food they furnish." Writing from Omaha, Nebraska, another officer, Lieutenant Colonel Albert Brackett, Second U.S. Cavalry, said the butchery was "as needless as it is cruel." Not only did it destroy a useful creature, it provoked Indian attacks.[33]

The ASPCA campaign reached the halls of Congress. Early in 1874, as hidemen flooded into Texas, Congress passed a bill making it illegal for anyone other than an Indian to kill a buffalo. Yet Columbus Delano, secretary of the interior, was dead-set against the bill. The

Headquarters for the American Society for the Prevention of Cruelty to Animals in New York City. The horse's statue above the main entrance indicates the society's original purpose of protecting workhorses.

buffalo, he told President Ulysses S. Grant, did not deserve to survive. "They eat the grass. They trample upon the plains. They are as uncivilized as the Indian." Grant refused to sign the bill into law.[34]

By 1887, buffalo had disappeared everywhere in the United States except Yellowstone National Park; illegal hunters quickly reduced the park's herd of two hundred to twenty-one. Private citizens and zoos owned another 256 buffalo. A few ranchers in Texas and Montana—Samuel Walking Coyote, Michael Pablo, Charles Goodnight, Charles "Buffalo" Jones—kept buffalo as a sideline to their cattle business. They tried (unsuccessfully) to weave buffalo hair into cloth, sell buffalo to zoos, and charge sportsmen up to one thousand dollars to shoot what had become the rarest of big-game animals. Even so, their herds, protected by cowboys toting six-shooters, increased. By 1902, there were more than seven hundred buffalo in private herds in the United States, and another five hundred fifty in Canada.[35]

As the twentieth century dawned, attitudes toward wild animals and wilderness were changing. By then, most Americans no longer lived on farms or in small towns, but in cities. People like William T. Hornaday, director of the Bronx Zoo in New York, felt that Americans must recapture the experience of living on the frontier, close to nature. Helping them do so had made Buffalo Bill a fortune. The mission of his Wild West show, the ex-hunter explained, was to teach city folks about the winning of the West. Usually, his shows included a buffalo exhibit. Seeing buffalo always brought cries of *ooh* and *ah* from the audience. For countless Americans, then, the onetime Lord of the Plains came to symbolize freedom and adventure.

William T. Hornaday with a bison calf.

Hornaday had friends in high places. One friend lived in the White House. Theodore Roosevelt, twenty-sixth president of the United States, was no ordinary politician. "Teddy," as Americans called him, was a famous naturalist. A world authority on birds, he studied land animals as well; a type of deer was named in his honor. But he was also a trophy hunter like Sir George Gore. Unlike Gore, however, Roosevelt demanded that hunters act in the right way and in the right spirit. That meant following a wounded animal to end its suffering and sparing pregnant females and the young. People should hunt, he said, for the same reason they climb mountains and explore distant lands. These were personal challenges, ways of testing their skill and courage. True hunters respected nature and wanted to protect it from "game butchers."[36]

Theodore Roosevelt and his family in 1898. Although an avid conservationist, Teddy was also a noted big-game hunter. He shot scores of grizzly bears and mountain lions in America, and elephants and lions in Africa.

Roosevelt did more than any other president, before or since, to protect America's natural heritage. He created scores of national parks, forest reserves, game preserves, and bird sanctuaries. With Roosevelt's encouragement, on December 1, 1905, Hornaday called a meeting in the Lion House of the Bronx Zoo. The meeting ended with the formation of the American Bison Society. The society's program called for the government to set aside land, stock it with buffalo, and guard them from hunters. Hornaday was the society's president, Roosevelt its honorary president. Its members were a select group of bankers, industrialists, and educators. People like these could get things done.

The society made an offer too good for Congress to refuse. If

Congress provided the land, Hornaday would stock it with buffalo from the Bronx Zoo's collection. Congress accepted. On October 11, 1907, seven bulls and eight cows arrived by rail at the Wichita National Forest and Game Preserve in Oklahoma. Local Indians were thrilled. Chief Quanah Parker, a famous Comanche leader, welcomed them at the depot. Mounted braves pointed them out to their children, who until then had only heard about the sacred animal, but had never seen one. Instantly, all the stories came to life.

Wichita National Forest and Game Preserve, Oklahoma. All the bison shown in this photograph are descendants of those sent by the American Bison Society.

A caged buffalo bull awaits shipment from the Bronx Zoo to the National Bison Range in Montana.

Soon afterward, the society persuaded Congress to create the National Bison Range in Montana. Congress gladly gave the land; the nation owned plenty of that. But money was something else, and lawmakers refused to give a cent to purchase buffalo. Since the Bronx Zoo had no more buffalo to spare, someone would have to buy them from ranchers.

The society began a nationwide fund-raising drive. Americans were used to such drives; the most recent, in 1885, had raised money to build the pedestal of the Statue of Liberty. Money to buy buffalo poured in, mostly from Easterners. Children gave pennies. Businesspeople wrote checks for hundreds of dollars.

In October 1909, at a cost of ten thousand dollars, thirty-four buffalo returned to Montana. William Hornaday was there. "As the crates were opened," he wrote with pride, "the bison backed out of them, looked about for a moment, [and] saw their Paradise Regained . . . the richest and the most beautiful grazing ground ever trodden by bison hoofs." By 1913, the society had spurred the government to create two more buffalo preserves—Fort Niobrara, Nebraska, and Wind Cave National Game Preserve in the Black Hills of South Dakota.[37]

Protected by the government, the herds steadily grew. By 1929, 3,385 buffalo lived in the United States. Having saved the Lord of the Plains, the American Bison Society abolished itself the following year. Since then, the buffalo has made a dramatic comeback. In 2000, the last year for which we have accurate figures, the country had 262,750. Most (244,000) are privately owned; the rest are in government (10,000) and American Indian herds (8,000). Zoos house another 750.

Why are so many in private hands? The answer is simple: money. Twenty-first-century America is a profitable market for all kinds of buffalo products. Those seeking to recapture the spirit of the old West can buy mementos from stores like Thundering Head Buffalo Products of Reno, Nevada, which charges up to $2,600 for a mounted head and $950

Logo for the Buffalo Guys of Elk Mountain, Wyoming. Buffalo ranching has become a big business in a diet-conscious nation. Like other ranchers, the Buffalo Guys specialize in buffalo hot dogs, buffalo jerky, buffalo steaks, and buffalo burgers, all from grass-fed, hormone-free animals.

for a robe. Yet, in a nation that is increasingly health-conscious, the largest market is for meat. Buffalo meat is more nutritious than beef, something Plains Indians and mountain men learned from experience long before scientists found the reasons. Today, ranchers slaughter roughly 20,000 buffalo each year in the United States, compared with 135,000 cattle slaughtered each day.

Although we have saved the buffalo, we cannot undo the events that brought them to the edge of extinction. The herds that once roamed the Great Plains are gone, never to return. Nor will the vast majority of today's (and tomorrow's) buffalo ever be as wild as they once were. The only wild herds are in national parks; they live without any human interference. Yet such parks are really protected islands in a sea of cattle ranches. Any buffalo that wander outside the parks are fair game, particularly since they may carry brucellosis, a disease that infects cattle. During the severe winter of 1996–1997, ranchers shot more than one thousand buffalo that had left Yellowstone National Park in search of food.

Moreover, in the last century, ranch buffalo have become very different from their wild cousins. While both look alike, ranch buffalo are changing. Long before recorded history, people domesticated wild animals and plants, that is, shaped them to live close to humans and to serve their needs.

Ranchers have shaped their buffalo by deciding which would become parents of the next generation. For example, they wanted buffalo that would not waste energy (and lose weight) fighting or running about.

Ranchers herd buffalo as cowboys still herd cattle. The buffalo shown here are domesticated; otherwise they would not let the herders get anywhere near them.

They preferred placid creatures that produced lots of meat. To get these, they allowed only buffalo with these traits to mate. Slowly, over many generations, the wilder animals disappeared, leaving only calmer ones. Today more than ninety percent of buffalo have become domesticated. Wildlife expert Dale F. Lott has called these "buffattle." As tame and meaty as cattle, and their horns cut off for safety, they are meek imitations of the animals Plains hunters had known.[38]

For thousands of years the buffalo was the keystone animal on the Plains. Their urine, dung, blood, and carcasses returned to nourish the earth. So did the urine, dung, blood, and carcasses of the other creatures—prairie dogs, wolves, birds, insects. All these creatures nourished the grasses, enabling them to thrive. However, the end of the herds affected everything that depended on them. Each year, native animals and plants became fewer. Cattle ranchers made matters worse. Unlike the buffalo, whose cup-shaped hooves shift the soil as they graze, allowing air to circulate, cattle hooves compress it, hardening it and reducing its fertility. To protect their cattle, ranchers nearly wiped out the predators—wolves, coyotes, bears. To plant wheat and corn, farmers plowed under the native grasses and poisoned prairie dogs.

Nature took its revenge. "Grass is what counts," a Texas rancher once said. "Grass is what holds the earth together." Eliminating the native grasses meant that their roots no longer bound the soil. The trouble begins whenever the rains fail to come on time, or fall enough, as they often do on the Plains. In 1886, rain hardly fell at all. For most of that year, the blazing sun baked the land. After ten long years of drought, the rains returned in 1896. Yet the worst still lay ahead. During the Dust Bowl years of the 1930s, drought and heat turned

Buffalo, under low-hanging storm clouds, roam the Black Hills of South Dakota.

When residents could no longer earn a living, they abandoned their farms, ranches, and towns. All Great Plains states have ghost towns like the one shown here.

exposed soil to dust. As a result, the wind blew it away. For nearly a decade, immense dust clouds called black blizzards blotted out the sun, buried farms, and destroyed the land's fertility.

Today, some Plains areas are in steep decline. The numbers tell a sad tale. More than a hundred counties, from the Dakotas to Texas, have suffered serious population losses. In some places, the population has slipped back to frontier level, defined as less than two persons per square mile. Kansas has hundreds of ghost towns, once-prosperous places with empty houses, caved-in roofs, and weed-choked streets. Nebraska has some ten thousand abandoned farms.

In the 1980s, scientist Frank J. Popper and his wife, Deborah E. Popper, called the settlement of the Great Plains "the largest, longest-running agricultural and environmental miscalculation in American history." The Poppers urged the creation of a Buffalo Commons in the empty counties, an open range where the buffalo could roam freely and

Scene from an experimental Great Plains Buffalo Commons created by Frank and Deborah Popper. By returning buffalo to their natural habitat, the Poppers hope to preserve the environment and encourage tourism in areas suffering from decades-old economic downturn.

the original plant life could come back. Returning its keystone animal to the Plains, they said, would revive the entire ecology, creating a vast national park and attracting tourist dollars from all over the world. (More Americans travel to see wildlife than view all professional sports events combined.) Although ranchers and farmers scorned the Poppers' idea at first, some have taken it up recently.[39]

Indians who had never heard of the Buffalo Commons were already creating their own versions of it on their reservations. "We recognize the bison as a symbol of our strength and unity, and that as we bring our herds back to health, we will also bring our people back to health," says Lakota scientist Fred DuBray. Restoring the buffalo is a way of reversing the damage to Indian health caused by generations of poverty. With diabetes and heart disease rampant on reservations, returning buffalo meat to the diet would go a long way toward improving Indians' overall health.[40]

What is more important, Indians see restoring the buffalo as key to their spiritual renewal. "Just having these animals around, knowing what they meant to our ancestors, and bringing kids out to connect with them has done wonders," says Mike Faith, who manages the buffalo herd on a Lakota reservation. The buffalo remind youngsters of how their people once lived, free and in harmony with nature.[41]

Indians began to bring back the buffalo in the 1930s. With surplus

Bison herd in Yellowstone National Park. As in all national parks, the animals shown here are wild. Park employees do nothing to feed them, inoculate them against disease, or protect them from predators such as wolves. In this way, the strongest survive to breed the next generation.

animals from the national parks, the Lakota and the Crow founded herds on their reservations in South Dakota and Montana. These reservations, incidentally, are still mostly covered with grama and buffalo grass. In 1990, eight tribes took a giant step forward when they formed the Intertribal Bison Cooperative (ITBC). Its aim, they explained, is "to restore bison to Indian Nations in a manner that is compatible with their spiritual and cultural beliefs and practices." In other words, they want the buffalo to be a constant, living presence in their daily lives. Today, fifty-one peoples belong to the ITBC. Altogether, its members have more than eight thousand buffalo in their herds.

So, despite all that has happened, the buffalo have survived. Yet things are not as they were, nor can they ever be. The herds that once thundered across the Great Plains are gone forever. Whether the survivors will continue to be anything like their wild ancestors is for us to decide. In making that decision, we can have no better guide than the wisdom of the White Buffalo Woman. For "we are as one: earth, sky, all living things, the two-legged, the four-legged, the winged ones, the trees, the grasses."

Buffalo herd roaming at sunset. There are many calves, a sign that this is probably a cow group.

GLOSSARY

Agriculture – farming

Brucellosis – an infection or disease caused by bacteria

Carcass – the body of a dead animal

Domesticate – to tame something so it can live with or be used by human beings

Dung – the feces of an animal

Ecology – the study of the relationship among plants, animals, and their environment

Ecosystem – a community of animals and plants interacting with their environment

Erosion – the gradual wearing away of a substance by water or wind

Fertility – plentiful plant growth

Great Spirit – in American Indian culture, a supernatural being who is worshiped

Grub – a soft, thick, wormlike larva of an insect

Impound – to shut up or confine in an area

Irrigation – supplying water to crops by artificial means, such as channels or pipes

Jackrabbit – a large hare, common in the western United States. It has very long ears and strong back legs for leaping.

Keystone species – a kind of animal or plant that is essential to making its ecosystem function well

Maize – corn

Missionary – someone who is sent by a church or religious group to teach that group's faith

Molten rock – lava

Nomads – groups of people who wander around instead of living in one place

Nuisance – someone or something that annoys you and causes problems for you

Paunch – belly

Pemmican – food consisting of lean meat that is dried, pounded, and mixed with melted fat

Prairie turnip – a plant common to the prairie used for medicine and food

Pronghorn – a fast-moving mammal common to the western prairie, also called pronghorn antelope

Quicksand – loose, wet sand that you can sink into

Ravine – a deep, narrow valley with steep sides

Ruminant – chewing the cud

Rut – the time when some mammals mate

Sanctuaries – natural areas where birds or animals are protected from hunters

Sinew – a strong fiber or band of tissue that connects a muscle to a bone, also called tendon

Skids – runners on the bottom of a sled or other vehicle

Stampede – a sudden, wild rush in one direction usually caused by something frightening

Tannery – a place where hides are made into leather by drying and curing

Thatch – a roof covering made from straw or reeds

Thunderbird – a bird that causes lightning and thunder in American Indian myth

Travois – a simple vehicle made of two poles with a platform or net between them for carrying things. The poles are tied to a dog or horse.

Vegetation – the plants that cover an area

Wanton – for no reason or provocation

Willow – a kind of tree

TEXT SOURCE NOTES

[1] Walter Prescott Webb, *The Great Plains* (Boston: Ginn and Company, 1931), 22.

[2] Wayne Gard, *The Great Buffalo Hunt* (New York: Alfred A. Knopf, 1960), 7.

[3] David A. Dary, *The Buffalo Book: The Full Saga of the American Animal* (Athens, OH: Swallow Press/Ohio University Press, 1989), 38–39.

[4] Tom McHugh, *The Time of the Buffalo* (New York: Alfred A. Knopf, 1972), 244, 245–246; Dary, *The Buffalo Book*, 39.

[5] Valerius Geist, *Buffalo Nation: History and Legend of the North American Bison* (Stillwater, MN: Voyageur Press, 1996), 63–67.

[6] McHugh, *The Time of the Buffalo*, 238.

[7] Gard, *The Great Buffalo Hunt*, 14.

[8] McHugh, *The Time of the Buffalo*, 14–16; Martin S. Garretson, *The American Bison: The Story of Its Extermination as a Wild Species and Its Restoration Under Federal Protection* (New York: New York Zoological Society, 1938), 60.

[9] Bruce Nelson, *The Land of the Dacotahs* (Minneapolis: University of Minnesota Press,1946),15–16.

[10] Shepard Krech, *The Ecological Indian: Myth and History* (New York: W. W. Norton & Co., 1999), 132.

[11] George Catlin, *Letters and Notes on the Manners, Customs, and Conditions of the North American Indians* (2 vols., New York: Dover, 1973), I, 127–128.

[12] McHugh, *The Time of the Buffalo*, 65.

[13] Andrew C. Isenberg, *The Destruction of the Bison: An Environmental History, 1750–1920* (Cambridge, MA: Cambridge University Press, 2000), 82; Krech, *The Ecological Indian*, 132.

[14] Isenberg, *The Destruction of the Bison*, 85; Geist, *Buffalo Nation*, 26, 47–48.

[15] McHugh, *The Time of the Buffalo*, 109.

[16] Geist, *Buffalo Nation*, 37; Ernest Callenbach, *Bring Back the Buffalo: A Sensible Future for America's Great Plains* (Washington, DC: Island Press, 1996), 65; McHugh, *The Time of the Buffalo*, 136–137.

[17] Dary, *The Buffalo Book*, 52.

[18] McHugh, *The Time of the Buffalo*, 78.

[19] Catlin, *Letters and Notes*, I, 200–201.

[20] Remi Nateau, *Fort Laramie and the Sioux Indians* (Englewood Cliffs, NJ: Prentice-Hall,1967), 50; Francis Haines, *The Buffalo*, (Norman, OK: University of Oklahoma Press, 1995), 143.

[21] Frank G. Roe, *The North American Buffalo* (Toronto: University of Toronto Press, 1972), 555.

[22] William T. Hornaday, *The Extermination of the American Bison* (Washington, DC: Smithsonian Institution Press, 2002), 487.

[23] McHugh, *The Time of the Buffalo*, 247.

[24] Carl Coke Rister, *The Southwestern Frontier*, 1865–1881 (Cleveland: The Arthur H. Clark Company, 1928), 225–226.

[25] Don Russell, *The Lives and Legends of Buffalo Bill* (Norman, OK: University of Oklahoma Press, 1969), 90.

[26] Gard, *The Great Buffalo Hunt*, 223.

[27] Haines, *The Buffalo*, 196.

[28] David D. Smits, "The Army and the Destruction of the Buffalo, 1865–1883," *Western Historical Quarterly 25* (1991), 335.

[29] Frank H. Mayer and Charles B. Roth, *The Buffalo Harvest* (Denver: Sage Books, 1958), 29–30.

[30] Hornaday, *The Extermination of the American Bison*, 503.

[31] Dary, *The Buffalo Book*, 120.

[32] Colin G. Calloway, ed., *Our Hearts Fell to the Ground: Plains Indian Views of How the West Was Lost* (New York: St. Martin's Press, 1996), 122–123.

[33] E. Douglas Branch, *The Hunting of the Buffalo* (Lincoln: University of Nebraska Press, 1962), 179. See also John J. Loeper, *Crusade for Kindness: Henry Bergh and the ASPCA* (New York: Atheneum, 1991).

[34] Branch, *The Hunting of the Buffalo,* 183.

[35] McHugh, *The Time of the Buffalo,* 294; Frank Graham, Jr., *Man's Dominion: The Story of Conservation in America* (Philadelphia: J. B. Lippincott Company, 1971), 113; Dary, *The Buffalo Book,* 234.

[36] Edward Wagenknecht, *The Seven Worlds of Theodore Roosevelt* (New York: Longmans, Green & Co., 1958), 17–18.

[37] McHugh, *The Time of the Buffalo,* 302.

[38] Lott, Dale F. et al. *American Bison: A Natural History,* (Berkeley, CA: University of California Press, 2002.)

[39] Callenbach, *Bring Back the Buffalo,* 88; Timothy Egan, "As Others Abandon the Plains, Indians and Bison Come Back," *The New York Times,* May 27, 2001.

[40] http://www.intertribalbison.org

[41] Egan, "As Others Abandon the Plains. . . ."

FOR MORE INFORMATION

BOOKS FOR YOUNG PEOPLE

Berman, Ruth. *American Bison*. Minneapolis, MN: Carolrhoda Books, 1992.

Hofsinde, Robert. *The Indian and the Buffalo*. New York: Morrow, 1961.

Hoyt-Goldsmith, Diane. *Buffalo Days*. New York: Holiday House, 1997.

Lepthein, Emilie. *Buffalo*. Chicago: Childrens Press, 1989.

Patent, Dorothy Hinshaw. *Buffalo: The American Bison Today*. New York: Clarion Books, 1986.

Robbins, Ken. *Thunder on the Plains: The Story of the American Buffalo*. New York: Simon and Schuster, 2001.

Swanson, Diane. *Buffalo Sunrise: The Story of a North American Giant*. San Francisco, CA: Sierra Club Books for Children, 1996.

Taylor, J. David. *The Bison and the Great Plains*. New York: Crabtree Publishing, 1990.

Winner, Cherie. *Bison*. Minnetonka, MN: NorthWord Press, 2001.

Ziter, Cary B. *The Moon of Falling Leaves: The Great Buffalo Hunt*. New York: Franklin Watts, 1988.

BOOKS FOR ADULTS

Barness, Larry. *The Bison in Art*. Fort Worth: Amon Carter Museum of Western Art, 1977.

Branch, E. Douglas. *The Hunting of the Buffalo*. Lincoln: University of Nebraska Press, 1962.

Callenbach, Ernest. *Bring Back the Buffalo: A Sensible Future for America's Great Plains*. Washington, DC: Island Press, 1996.

Catlin, George. *Letters and Notes on the Manners, Customs, and Conditions of the North American Indians*. 2 vols., New York: Dover, 1973. This book was first published in 1844.

Dary, David A. *The Buffalo Book: The Full Saga of the American Animal*. Athens, OH: Swallow Press/Ohio University Press, 1989.

Erdoes, Richard, and Alfonso Ortiz, eds., *American Indian Myths and Legends*. New York: Pantheon Books, 1984.

Gard, Wayne. *The Great Buffalo Hunt*. New York: Alfred A. Knopf, 1960.

Garretson, Martin S. *The American Bison: The Story of Its Extermination as a Wild Species and Its Restoration Under Federal Protection*. New York: New York Zoological Society, 1938.

Geist, Valerius. *Buffalo Nation: History and Legend of the North American Bison*. Stillwater, MN: Voyageur Press, 1996.

Goble, Paul. *The Legend of the White Buffalo Woman*. Washington, DC: National Geographic Society, 1998.

Graham, Frank, Jr. *Man's Dominion: The Story of Conservation in America.* Philadelphia: J. B. Lippincott Company, 1971.

Haines, Francis. *The Buffalo: The Story of the American Bison and Their Hunters from Prehistoric Times to the Present*. Norman, OK: University of Oklahoma Press, 1995.

Hornaday, William T. *The Extermination of the American Bison.* Washington, DC: Smithsonian Institution Press, 2002. Published originally in Smithsonian Reports for 1887, Part II, published in 1889.

Isenberg, Andrew C. *The Destruction of the Bison: An Environmental History, 1750–1920.* Cambridge, MA: Cambridge University Press, 2000.

Krech, Shepard. *The Ecological Indian: Myth and History*. New York: W. W. Norton & Co., 1999.

Loeper, John J. *Crusade for Kindness: Henry Bergh and the ASPCA.* New York: Atheneum, 1991.

Trefethen, James B. *An American Crusade for Wildlife*. New York: Winchester Press and the Boone and Crockett Club, 1975.

Wagenknecht, Edward. *The Seven Worlds of Theodore Roosevelt.* New York: Longmans, Green & Co., 1958.

Webb, Walter Prescott. *The Great Plains*. Boston: Ginn and Company, 1931.

WEB SITES

ASPCA'S Animaland: American Society for the Prevention of Cruelty to Animals
http://www.animaland.org

Animal Diversity Web: University of Michigan Museum of Zoology
http://animaldiversity.ummz.umich.edu/index.html

Cyber Zoo
lsb.syr.edu/projects/cyberzoo/americanbison.html

Animals A to Z: Oakland Zoo
http://www.oaklandzoo.org/atoz/atoz.html

Kids' Planet
http://www.kidsplanet.org

Kids Go Wild: The Wildlife Conservation Society
http://wcs.org/7490/kidsgowild

National Parks Conservation Association
www.npca.org

NatureWorks: New Hampshire Public Television
www.nhptv.org/natureworks/americanbison.htm

INDEX

IMAGE SOURCE NOTES

Page 2: Darrell Gulin/CORBIS; page 6: The New York Public Library/ART RESOURCE; page 8: Hornaday, *The Extermination of the American Bison*, 1889 ACM Library; page 9: Larry Lee Photography/CORBIS; pages 10–11: 1964.93-Meyers Strauss/Amon Carter Museum, TX; page 13 (top): W. Perry Conway/CORBIS; page 13 (bottom): George D. Lepp/CORBIS; page 15: William Manning/CORBIS; pages 16–17: Smithsonian American Art Museum, Washington, D.C./ART RESOURCE; page 18: RF/CORBIS; page 20: Smithsonian Institute, Department of Mammals; page 22: Layne Kennedy/CORBIS; page 23: NGS/GETTYIMAGES, NYC; page 25: CORBIS; page 27: Jim Brandenburg/MINDEN PICTURES; page 28: Layne Kennedy/CORBIS; page 29: Lowell Georgia/CORBIS; pages 30–31: Jim Brandenburg /MINDEN PICTURES; page 32: North Wind Picture Archives, Alfred, ME; page 33: Jim Brandenburg/MINDEN PICTURES; page 34: 1961.135-Charles M. Russell/Amon Carter Museum, TX; page 37: Burstein Collection/ CORBIS; page 38: Denver Public Library X-33185; page 41: The Granger Collection, NYC; page 42: Geoffrey Clements/CORBIS; page 43: Werner Forman/ART RESOURCE; page 45: Private Collection/Bridgeman Art Library; page 46: Private Collection, The Stapleton Collection/Bridgeman Art Library; pages 48–49: Walters Art Museum/Bridgeman Art Library; page 49: Paul A. Souders/CORBIS; page 51: Private Collection, Bultin Picture Library/Bridgeman Art Library; page 52: Minnesota Historical Society, LOC # E97.32r9 Neg#67258; pages 54–55: The Granger Collection, NYC; page 55: Peabody Essex Museum/Bridgeman Art Library; page 56: Werner Forman/ART RESOURCE; page 57: Smithsonian American Art Museum/ART RESOURCE; page 58: Geoffrey Clements/CORBIS; page 60: Charles M. Russell/The Gund Collection of Western Art, NJ; page 62: Smithsonian American Art Museum/ART RESOURCE; page 63: CORBIS; pages 64–65: Smithsonian American Art Museum/ART RESOURCE; page 67: The Granger Collection, NYC; page 68: Smithsonian American Art Museum/ART RESOURCE; page 70: DeGolyer Library, Southern Methodist University, Ag 1982.0086.60, Dallas, TX; page 72: The Huffman Collection/The Montana Historical Society; page 73: The Granger Collection, NYC; pages 74–75: Denver Public Library X-21874; page 77: Bettmann/CORBIS; page 78: North Wind Picture Archives, Alfred, ME; pages 80–81: North Wind Picture Archives, Alfred, ME; page 83: CORBIS; page 84: W. E. Webb, Buffalo Land, E. Hannaford, Chicago & Cincinnati, 1872; page 85: Bettmann/CORBIS; page 87: Leonard de Salva/CORBIS; page 88: The Huffman Collection # 981-013/The Montana Historical Society; page 89: University of Oklahoma, Western History Collection-Hensley.Claude; page 91: Denver Public Library X-33743; page 93: Burton Historical Collection/Detroit Public Library; page 95: Werner Forman/ART RESOURCE; page 96: Layne Kennedy/CORBIS; page 97: Hulton Archive/GETTYIMAGES; page 99: CORBIS; page 101: Smithsonian Institute Archives # 74-12338; page 102: CORBIS; page 103: Wichita Mountain Wildlife Refuge/U.S. Fish & Wildlife Service; page 104: American Bison Society; page 106: www.thebuffaloguys.com; page 107: Layne Kennedy/CORBIS; page 109: David McNew/GETTYIMAGES; page 110: Phil Schermeister/CORBIS; page 111: Great Plains Restoration Council, Fort Worth, TX; page 113: Jeff Vanuga/CORBIS; pages 114–115: Layne Kennedy/CORBIS.